SO-BZX-262

Fodor's 98 Pocket San Francisco

Reprinted from *Fodor's San Francisco '98*

Fodor's Travel Publications, Inc.
New York • Toronto • London • Sydney • Auckland
www.fodors.com/

Fodor's Pocket San Francisco

EDITORS: Christina Knight and Amy McConnell

Editorial Contributors: Robert Andrews, Vincent Bielski, David Brown, Tara Duggan, Dennis Harvey, Patrick Hoctel, Heidi Sarna, Helayne Schiff, M. T. Schwartzman (Essential Information editor), Julene Snyder, Dinah A. Spritzer, Sharon Silva, Sharron Wood

Editorial Production: Stacey Kulig

Maps: David Lindroth, *cartographer*; Steven K. Amsterdam, *map editor*

Design: Fabrizio La Rocca, *creative director*; Lyndell Brookhouse-Gil, *cover design*; Jolie Novak, *photo editor*

Production/Manufacturing: Mike Costa

Cover Photograph: Phil Schermeister/Photographers/Aspen

Copyright

Special Sales

Fodor's Travel Publications are available at special discounts for bulk purchases for sales promotions or premiums. Special editions can be created in large quantities for special needs. For more information, contact Special Markets, Fodor's Travel Publications, 201 East 50th Street, New York, NY 10022. Inquiries from Canada should be directed to Random House of Canada, Ltd., Marketing Dept., 1265 Aerowood Dr., Mississauga, Ont. L4W 1B9. Inquiries from the United Kingdom should be sent to Fodor's Travel Publications, 20 Vauxhall Bridge Road, London SW1V 2SA, England.

CONTENTS

Index *157*

Maps

ON THE ROAD WITH FODOR'S

WE'RE ALWAYS thrilled to get letters from readers, especially one like this:

It took us an hour to decide what book to buy and we now know we picked the best one. Your book was wonderful, easy to follow, very accurate, and good on pointing out eating places, informal as well as formal. When we saw other people using your book, we would look at each other and smile.

Our editors and writers are deeply committed to making every Fodor's guide "the best one"—not only accurate but always charming, brimming with sound recommendations and solid ideas, right on the mark in describing restaurants and hotels, and full of fascinating facts that make you view what you've traveled to see in a rich new light.

About Our Writers

Our success in achieving our goals—and in helping to make your trip the best of all possible vacations—is a credit to the hard work of our extraordinary writers and our San Francisco–born editor, Amy McConnell.

Exploring updater **Vincent Bielski,** who has lived in seven neighborhoods during his 15 years in San Francisco, is a contributor to *San Francisco Focus, Hippocrates,* and *California Lawyer.*

Outdoor Activities updater **Tara Duggan** gained an insider's perspective of the Bay Area sports scene during her tenure on the staff of "Bay Sports Review." She relishes her weekend treks along San Francisco's beaches.

Dining updater **Sharon Silva** has been dining and writing her way through the San Francisco Bay Area for some 20 years and is a regular contributor to *San Francisco Focus* magazine.

Updating Nightlife and the Arts was a breeze for **Julene Snyder,** former music editor of the *S.F. Weekly.* A longtime resident of San Francisco, Julene also revamped the Shopping chapter and Essential Information.

After reviewing San Francisco's best hotels and B&Bs, Lodging updater **Sharron Wood** will never be able to stay in a dumpy roadside motel again. A freelance travel writer and book editor, Sharron loves living in a city where there's so much to write about.

New This Year

This year we've added a chapter on Outdoor Activities that will guide your feet or wheels through the best scenic routes.

We're also proud to announce that the American Society of Travel Agents has endorsed Fodor's as its guidebook of choice. ASTA is the world's largest and most influential travel trade association, operating in more than 170 countries, with 27,000 members pledged to adhere to a strict code of ethics reflecting the Society's motto, "Integrity in Travel." ASTA shares Fodor's devotion to providing smart, honest travel information and advice to travelers, and we've long recommended that our readers consult ASTA member agents for the experience and professionalism they bring to the table.

On the Web, check out Fodor's site (www.fodors.com/) for information on major destinations around the world and travel-savvy interactive features. The Web site also lists the 85-plus stations nationwide that carry the Fodor's Travel Show, a live call-in program that airs every weekend. Tune in to hear guests discuss their wonderful adventures—or call in to get answers for your most pressing travel questions.

New and Noteworthy

The renaissance of South of Market Street (SoMa) continues, as new shops, galleries, and museums join the area's flagship cultural institutions. The nearby **Moscone Convention Center** is slated for expansion over the next few years; the roof of Moscone South will be the foundation of a children's center, scheduled to open in 1998. Also included will be a studio for technology and the arts, an ice-skating rink, day-care center, children's gardens, and a 1903 Charles Looff carousel, formerly at Playland at the Beach.

The 4-mi, well-marked **Barbary Coast Trail** winds its way from SoMa to the Northern Waterfront past 50 sites from the city's wild gold-rush days. For information about the trail, pick up a brochure at the San Francisco Visitors Information Center; the most interesting sites begin near Jackson Square.

Performing arts organizations began to return to their homes in 1997 after being seismically upgraded. As we headed to press in summer 1997, the **War Memorial Opera House** was scheduled to open in September 1997.

At Ocean Beach the Willis Polk–designed **Beach Chalet,** closed since the 1970s, reopened in 1997. The ground floor has a Golden Gate Park visitor center and a wraparound Work Projects Administration mural depicting San Francisco in the 1930s. Upstairs, a brew pub–restaurant has become an instant hit.

Seventeen historic F-line street cars chug up and down the length of **Market Street,** harkening back to another time. The cars are painted in the livery of their cities of origin: many hail from the United States, but there are also cars from Blackpool, England, and Milan, Italy. Designed in the 1920s and '30s, the cars are a pleasure to ride. The fare is the same as for the more modern buses.

How to Use This Book

Organization

Up front is **Essential Information,** an easy-to-use section divided alphabetically by topic. Under each listing you'll find tips and information that will help you accomplish what you need to in San Francisco. You'll also find addresses and telephone numbers of organizations and companies that offer destination-related services and detailed information.

The first chapter, **Destination: San Francisco,** helps get you in the mood for your trip, and Festivals and Seasonal Events alerts you to just some of the many special events in San Francisco.

The **Exploring** chapter is subdivided by neighborhood and lists each neighborhood's sights alphabetically. The remaining chapters are arranged in alphabetical order by subject (dining, lodging, nightlife and the arts, outdoor activities, and shopping).

Icons and Symbols

★   Our special recommendations
✕   Restaurant
🏠 Lodging establishment
☾   Good for kids (rubber duckie)
☞   Sends you to another section of the guide for more information
⊠   Address
☎   Telephone number
☾   Opening and closing times
🎫 Admission prices (those we give apply to adults; substantially reduced fees are often available for children, students, and senior citizens)

Numbers in black circles that appear on the maps and in the margins correspond to one another.

Credit Cards

The following abbreviations are used: **AE,** American Express; **D,** Discover; **DC,** Diners Club; **MC,** MasterCard; and **V,** Visa.

Please Write to Us

You can use this book in the confidence that all prices and opening times are based on information supplied to us at press time; Fodor's cannot accept responsibility for any errors. Time inevitably brings changes, so always confirm information when it matters—especially if you're making a detour to visit a specific place. In addition, when making reservations be sure to mention if you have a disability or are traveling with children, if you prefer a private bath or a certain type of bed, or if you have specific dietary needs or other concerns.

Were the restaurants we recommended as described? Did our hotel picks exceed your expectations? Did you find a museum we recommended a waste of time? If you have complaints, we'll look into them and revise our entries when the facts warrant it. If you've discovered a special place that we haven't included, we'll pass the information along to our correspondents and have them check it out. So send us your feedback, positive *and* negative: email us at editors@fodors.com (specifying the name of the book on the subject line) or write the San Francisco editor at Fodor's, 201 East 50th Street, New York, NY 10022. Have a wonderful trip!

Karen Cure
Editorial Director

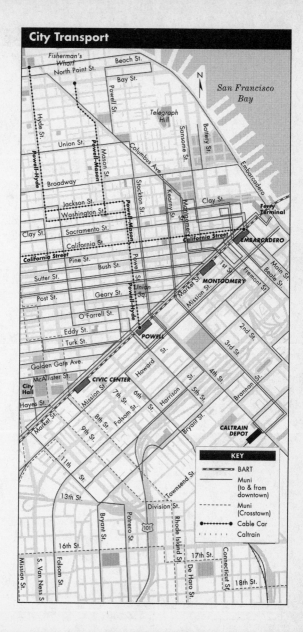

City Transport

Fisherman's Wharf

San Francisco Bay

Beach St.

North Point St.

Bay St.

Powell St.

Telegraph Hill

Union St.

Hyde St.

Powell-Hyde

Powell St.

Mason St.

Columbus Ave.

Sansome St.

Battery St.

Powell-Mason

Broadway

Stockton St.

Kearny St.

Montgomery St.

Clay St.

Embarcadero

Ferry Terminal

Jackson St.

Washington St.

Powell-Mason

Clay St.

Sacramento St.

California St.

California Street

EMBARCADERO

California Street

Pine St.

Powell St.

Bush St.

Powell-Hyde

1st St.

Fremont St.

Main St.

Beale St.

Sutter St.

Post St.

Geary St.

Union Sq.

Market St.

Mission St.

MONTGOMERY

O'Farrell St.

Eddy St.

Turk St.

POWELL

St.

2nd St.

3rd St.

Brannan St.

Golden Gate Ave.

McAllister St.

City Hall

CIVIC CENTER

Howard

St.

4th St.

5th St.

Hayes St.

Mission St.

7th St.

6th St.

St.

Harrison

St.

Market St.

8th St.

Folsom St.

9th St.

Bryant St.

CALTRAIN DEPOT

11th St.

13th St.

Division St.

Townsend St.

Rhode Island St.

Bryant St.

Potrero St.

101

16th St.

17th St.

Connecticut St.

S. Van Ness S

Mission St.

Folsom St.

De Haro St.

18th St.

KEY	
▬▬▬	BART
———	Muni (to & from downtown)
- - - -	Muni (Crosstown)
●●●●●	Cable Car
·····	Caltrain

San Francisco

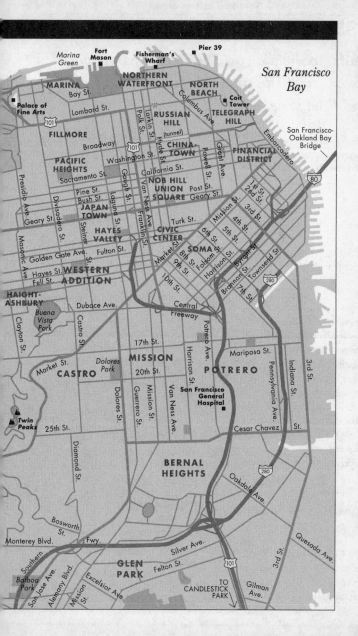

ESSENTIAL INFORMATION

Basic Information on Traveling in San Francisco, Savvy Tips to Make Your Trip a Breeze, and Companies and Organizations to Contact

AIR TRAVEL

MAJOR AIRLINE OR LOW-COST CARRIER?

Most people choose a flight based on price. Yet there are other issues to consider. Major airlines offer the greatest number of departures; smaller airlines—including regional, low-cost and no-frill airlines—usually have a more limited number of flights daily. Major airlines have frequent-flyer partners, which allow you to credit mileage earned on one airline to your account with another. Low-cost airlines offer a definite price advantage and fewer restrictions, such as advance-purchase requirements. Safety-wise, low-cost carriers as a group have a good history, but **check the safety record before booking** any low-cost carrier; call the Federal Aviation Administration's Consumer Hotline (☞ Complaints, *below*).

MAJOR AIRLINES➤ **America West** (☎ 800/235–9292) to Oakland, San Francisco. **American** (☎ 800/433–7300) to Oakland, San Francisco. **British Airways** (☎ 800/247–9297) to San Francisco. **Continental** (☎ 800/231–0856) to San Francisco. **Delta** (☎ 800/241–4141) to Oakland, San Francisco. **Northwest** (☎ 800/225–2525) to San Francisco. **Southwest** (☎ 800/435–9792) to San Francisco. **TWA** (☎ 800/892–4141) to San Francisco. **United** (☎ 800/538–2929) to Oakland, San Francisco. **US Airways** (☎ 800/428–4322) to San Francisco.

SMALLER AIRLINES➤ **Midwest Express** (☎ 800/452–2022) to San Francisco. **Reno Air** (☎ 800/736–6247) to San Francisco.

AIRLINE TICKETS➤ ☎ 800/FLY–4–LESS. ☎ 800/FLY–ASAP.

FROM THE U.K.➤ **British Airways** (☎ 0345/222–111). **United** (☎ 0800/888–555). **Virgin Atlantic** (☎ 01293/747–747). **American** (☎ 0345/789–789) flies via New York or Chicago, and **Delta** (☎ 0800/414–767) flies via Los Angeles or Cincinnati.

THE LOWEST FARE

The least-expensive airfares to San Francisco are priced for round-trip travel. Major airlines usually require that you **book in advance and buy the ticket within 24 hours,** and you may have to **stay over a Saturday night.** It's smart to **call a** number of airlines, and when you are quoted a good price, **book it on the spot**—the same fare may not be available on the same flight the next day. Airlines generally allow you to change your return date for a fee of $25–$50. If you don't use your ticket you can apply the cost toward the purchase of a new ticket, again for a small charge. However, most low-fare tickets are nonrefundable. To get the lowest airfare, **check different routings.** If your destination or home city has more than one gateway, compare prices to and from different airports. Also price off-peak flights, which may be significantly less expensive.

To save money on flights from the United Kingdom and back, **look into an APEX or Super-PEX ticket.** APEX tickets must be booked in advance and have certain restrictions. Super-PEX tickets can be purchased at the airport on the day of departure—subject to availability.

DON'T STOP UNLESS YOU MUST

When you book, **look for nonstop flights** and **remember that "direct" flights stop at least once.** Try to **avoid connecting flights,** which require a change of plane. Two airlines may jointly operate a connecting flight, so ask if your airline operates every segment—you may find that your preferred carrier flies you only part of the way.

AGENTS

Travel agents, especially those who specialize in finding the lowest fares can be especially helpful when booking a plane ticket. When you're quoted a price, **ask your agent if the price is likely to get any lower.** Good agents know the seasonal fluctuations of airfares and can usually anticipate a sale or fare war. However, waiting can be risky: The fare could go *up* as seats become scarce, and you may wait so long that your preferred flight sells out. A wait-and-see strategy works best if your plans are flexible, but if you must arrive and depart on certain dates, don't delay.

AVOID GETTING BUMPED

Airlines routinely overbook planes, knowing that not everyone with a ticket will show up, but sometimes everyone does. When that happens, airlines ask for volunteers to give up their seats. In return these volunteers usually get a certificate for a free flight and are rebooked on the next flight out. If there are not enough volunteers the airline must choose who will be denied boarding. The first to get bumped are passengers who checked in late and those flying on discounted tickets, **so get to the gate and check in as early as possible,** especially during peak periods.

Always **bring a photo ID to the airport.** You may be asked to show it before you are allowed to check in.

ENJOY THE FLIGHT

For better service, **fly smaller or regional carriers,** which often have higher passenger-satisfaction ratings. Sometimes you'll find leather seats, more legroom, and better food.

For more legroom, **request an emergency-aisle seat**; don't however, sit in the row in front of the emergency aisle or in front of a bulkhead, where seats may not recline.

To avoid jet lag try to maintain a normal routine while traveling. At night **get some sleep.** By day **eat light meals, drink water (not alcohol), and move about the cabin** to stretch your legs.

COMPLAINTS

If your baggage goes astray or your flight goes awry, complain right away. Most carriers require that you file a claim immediately.

AIRLINE COMPLAINTS➤ U.S. Department of Transportation **Aviation Consumer Protection Division** (✉ C-75, Washington, DC 20590, ☎ 202/366–2220). **Federal Aviation Administration (FAA) Consumer Hotline** (☎ 800/322–7873).

AIRPORTS & TRANSFERS

The major gateway to San Francisco is the **San Francisco International Airport,** just south of the city, off U.S. 101. Several domestic airlines serve the **Oakland Airport,** which is across the bay but not much farther away from downtown San Francisco (via I–880 and I–80), although traffic on the Bay Bridge may at times make travel time longer.

Flying time is six hours from New York, four hours from Chicago, and one hour from Los Angeles.

AIRPORT INFORMATION➤ **San Francisco International Airport** (☎ 650/761–0800). **Oakland Airport** (☎ 415/577–4000).

TRANSFERS

A taxi ride from the airport to downtown costs about $30. Airport shuttles are inexpensive and efficient. The SFO Airporter ($10) picks up passengers at baggage claim (lower level) and serves selected downtown hotels. Super-Shuttle stops at the upper-level traffic islands and takes you from the airport to anywhere within the city limits of San Francisco. It costs $12 for the first passenger, plus $8 for each additional passenger to the same destination.

TAXIS & SHUTTLES➤ **SFO Airporter** (☎ 415/495–8404). **Super-shuttle** (☎ 415/558–8500).

BART

You can use Bay Area Rapid Transit (BART) trains to reach Oakland, Berkeley, Concord, Richmond, Fremont, and Martinez; extensions are expected to open southeast to Castro Valley and Dublin. Trains also travel south from San Francisco as far as Daly City and Colma. Fares run from $1.10 to $4.45, and a $3.80 excursion ticket buys a three-county tour.

BART➤ **Bay Area Rapid Transit** ☎ 650/992–2278.

BUS TRAVEL

The San Francisco Municipal Railway System, or Muni, operates diesel and trolley buses, Metro streetcars, the F Market historic streetcar line, and the world–famous cable cars. The Metro streetcars operate in the Market St. Subway, one level above BART, and then operate on the street surface in outlying areas of the city. Muni provides 24-hour service to all areas of the city.

On buses and streetcars, the fare is $1. **Bring exact change;** dollar bills are accepted in the fare boxes. Transfers are issued free upon request at the time the fare is paid. They are valid for 90 minutes to two hours for two boardings of a bus or streetcar in any direction.

MUNI➤ **San Francisco Municipal Railway System,** or **Muni** (☎ 415/673–6864).

CABLE CARS

The sensation of coursing San Francisco's hills in a small, open-air, clanging conveyance make cable cars popular, crowded, and an experience to ride: Move toward one quickly as it pauses, wedge yourself into any available space, and hold on! The cars run a constant 9½ mph.

The fare (for one direction) is $2; transfers are neither issued nor accepted for cable car service. You can buy tickets on board (exact change is preferred) or at kiosks at a few major terminals such as the one at Powell and Market streets. Be wary of street people attempting to "help" you buy a ticket.

A $6 pass good for unlimited travel all day on all routes can be purchased on the cable cars. Also, one-day ($6), three-day ($10), or seven-day ($15) Passports can be purchased at several outlets, including the cable car ticket booth at Powell & Market and the Visitors Information Center downstairs in Hallidie Plaza. These Passports are good for unlimited Muni travel and for discounts at visitor attractions, including the museums in Golden Gate Park.

The Powell-Mason line and the Powell-Hyde line begin at Powell and Market streets near Union Square and terminate at Fisherman's Wharf. The California Street line runs east and west from Market Street near the Embarcadero to Van Ness Avenue.

CALTRAIN

CalTrain connects San Francisco to Palo Alto, San Jose, and Santa Clara. Trains leave the city at 4th and Townsend streets. One-way fares run $3.75–$4.75. Trips last 1–1½ hours.

CALTRAIN➤ CalTrain (☎ 800/660–4287).

CAR RENTAL

Unless you plan on making excursions into Marin County, the Wine Country, or Silicon Valley, **avoid renting a car.** Public transportation is ubiquitous and efficient; parking is terrible.

Rates in San Francisco begin at $36 a day and $123 a week for an economy car with air conditioning, an automatic transmission, and unlimited mileage. This does not include tax on car rentals, which is 8.25%.

MAJOR AGENCIES➤ **Alamo** (☎ 800/327–9633, 0800/272–2000 in the U.K.). **Avis** (☎ 800/331–1212, 800/879–2847 in Canada). **Budget** (☎ 800/527–0700, 0800/181181 in the U.K.). **Dollar** (☎ 800/800–4000; 0990/565656 in the U.K., where it is known as Eurodollar). **Hertz** (☎ 800/654–3131, 800/263–0600 in Canada, 0345/555888 in the U.K.). **National InterRent** (☎ 800/227–7368; 0345/222525 in the U.K., where it is known as Europcar InterRent).

LOCAL AGENCIES➤ San Francisco has a few budget rental-car companies, among the lowest-priced is **Reliable** (☎ 415/928–4414). At the other end of the price spectrum, **Sunbelt** (☎ 415/771–9191) specializes in BMWs and Corvette and Miata convertibles.

CUT COSTS

To get the best deal, **book through a travel agent who is willing to shop around.** When pricing cars, **ask about the location of the rental lot.** Some off-airport locations offer lower rates, and their lots are only minutes from the terminal via complimentary shuttle. You also may want to **price local car-rental companies,** whose rates may be lower still, although their service and maintenance may not be as good as those of a name-brand agency. Remember to ask about required deposits, cancellation penalties, and drop-off charges if you're planning to pick up the car in one city and leave it in another.

Also **ask your travel agent about a company's customer-service record.** How has it responded to late plane arrivals and vehicle mishaps? Are there often lines at the rental counter, and, if you're traveling during a holiday period, does a confirmed reservation guarantee you a car?

Be sure to **look into wholesalers,** companies that do not own fleets but rent in bulk from those that do and often offer better rates than traditional car-rental operations. Prices are best during off-peak periods.

RENTAL WHOLESALERS➤ **Auto Europe** (☎ 207/842–2000 or 800/223–5555, FAX 800/235–6321). The **Kemwel Group** (☎ 914/835–5555 or 800/678–0678, FAX 914/835–5126).

NEED INSURANCE?

When driving a rented car you are generally responsible for any damage to or loss of the vehicle. You also are liable for any property damage or personal injury that you may cause while driving. Before you rent, **see what coverage you already have** under the terms of your personal auto-insurance policy and credit cards.

For $9 a day (some states, including California, have capped the price), rental companies sell protection, known as a collision- or loss-damage waiver (CDW or LDW) that eliminates your liability for damage to the car; it's always optional and should never be automatically added to your bill.

In most states you don't need CDW if you have personal auto insurance or other liability insurance. However, **make sure you have enough coverage to pay for the car.** If you do not have auto insurance or an umbrella policy that covers damage to third parties, purchasing CDW or LDW is highly recommended.

BEWARE SURCHARGES

Before you pick up a car in one city and leave it in another, **ask about drop-off charges or one-way service fees,** which can be substantial. Note, too, that some rental agencies charge extra if you return the car before the time specified on your contract. To avoid a hefty refueling fee, **fill the tank just before you turn in the car,** but be aware that gas stations near the rental outlet may overcharge.

MEET THE REQUIREMENTS

In the United States you must be 21 to rent a car, and rates may be higher if you're under 25. You'll pay extra for child seats (about $3 per day), which are compulsory for children under five, and for additional drivers (about $2 per day). Residents of the U.K. will need a reservation voucher, a passport, a U.K. driver's license, and a travel policy that covers each driver, in order to pick up a car.

CUSTOMS & DUTIES

ENTERING THE U.S.

Visitors age 21 and over may import the following into the United States: 200 cigarettes or 50 cigars or 2 kilograms of tobacco, 1 liter of alcohol, and gifts worth $100. Prohibited items include meat products, seeds, plants, and fruits.

ENTERING CANADA

If you've been out of Canada for at least seven days you may bring in C$500 worth of goods duty-free. If you've been away for fewer than seven days but more than 48 hours, the duty-free allowance drops to C$200; if your trip lasts 24–48 hours, the allowance is C$50. You may not pool allowances with family members. Goods claimed under the C$500 exemption may follow you by mail; those claimed under the lesser exemptions must accompany you.

Alcohol and tobacco products may be included in the seven-day and 48-hour exemptions but not in the 24-hour exemption. If you meet the age requirements of the province or territory through which you reenter Canada you may bring in, duty-free, 1.14 liters (40 imperial ounces) of wine or liquor *or* 24 12-ounce cans or bottles of beer or ale. If you are 16 or older you may bring in, duty-free, 200 cigarettes and 50 cigars; these items must accompany you.

You may send an unlimited number of gifts worth up to C$60 each duty-free to Canada. Label the package UNSOLICITED GIFT—VALUE UNDER $60. Alcohol and tobacco are excluded.

INFORMATION➤ **Revenue Canada** (✉ 2265 St. Laurent Blvd. S, Ottawa, Ontario K1G 4K3, ☎ 613/993–0534, 800/461–9999 in Canada).

ENTERING THE U.K.
From countries outside the EU, including the United States, you may import, duty-free, 200 cigarettes or 50 cigars; 1 liter of spirits or 2 liters of fortified or sparkling wine or liqueurs; 2 liters of still table wine; 60 milliliters of perfume; 250 milliliters of toilet water; plus £136 worth of other goods, including gifts and souvenirs.

INFORMATION➤ **HM Customs and Excise** (✉ Dorset House, Stamford St., London SE1 9NG, ☎ 0171/202–4227).

DISABILITIES & ACCESSIBILITY

ACCESS IN SAN FRANCISCO
California is a national leader in making attractions and facilities accessible to travelers with disabilities. Since 1982, the state building code has required that all construction for public use include access for people with disabilities. State laws provide special privileges, such as license plates allowing special parking spaces, unlimited parking in time-limited spaces, and free parking in metered spaces. Identification from states other than California is honored.

LOCAL RESOURCES➤ The **San Francisco Convention and Visitors Bureau** (✉ Box 429097, San Francisco 94142–9097, ☎ 415/974–6900, TTY 415/392–0328) publishes a **San Francisco Lodging Guide** that spells out which hotels are up to ADA requirements. Write or call for a free copy. The **California State Coastal Conservancy** (✉ Publications Dept., 1330 Broadway, Suite 1100, Oakland 94612, ☎ 510/286–1015) publishes the free booklet "**Wheelchair Riders Guide to San Francisco Bay and Nearby Shorelines.**"

PARKS

The National Park Service provides a Golden Access Passport for all national parks free of charge to those who are medically blind or have a permanent disability; the passport covers the entry fee for the holder and anyone accompanying the holder in the same private vehicle as well as a 50% discount on camping and various other user fees. Apply for the passport in person at a national recreation facility that charges an entrance fee; proof of disability is required.

SUBWAYS

All stations in **Bay Area Rapid Transit** (BART) are equipped with elevators. Call the station agent on the white courtesy telephone. Stations also have wheelchair-accessible rest rooms, phones, and drinking fountains. For information on a **Bay Region Transit Discount Card**, call BART (☎ 650/992-2278).

EMERGENCIES

For **police, fire,** or **ambulance,** telephone 911.

HOSPITALS➤ Two hospitals with 24-hour emergency rooms are **San Francisco General Hospital** (⊠ 1001 Potrero Ave., ☎ 415/206-8000) and the **Medical Center at the University of California, San Francisco** (⊠ 505 Parnassus Ave. at 3rd Ave., near Golden Gate Park, ☎ 415/476-1000). **Physician Access Medical Center** (⊠ 26 California St., ☎ 415/397-2881) is a drop-in clinic in the Financial District, open weekdays 7:30 AM-5 PM. **Access Health Care** (☎ 415/565-6600) provides drop-in medical care at Davies Medical Center, Castro Street at Duboce Avenue, daily 8-8.

24-HOUR PHARMACIES➤ **Walgreens Drug Stores** have 24-hour pharmacies at 498 Castro at 18th St. (☎ 415/861-3136), 25 Point Lobos near 42nd Avenue and Geary Street (☎ 415/386-0736), and 3201 Divisadero Street at Lombard Street (☎ 415/931-6417). Downtown, the Walgreens pharmacy at 135 Powell Street near Market Street (☎ 415/391-7222) is open seven days a week from 8 AM-8 PM.

FERRY TRAVEL

Several ferry lines run out of San Francisco. **Golden Gate Ferry** runs service seven days a week to and from Sausalito and Larkspur, leaving from behind the San Francisco Ferry Building on the Embarcadero. **The Red and White Fleet** operates a number of lines, including a Golden Gate cruise, service to Alcatraz and Angel Island, ferries to Sausalito and Tiburon, and private tours; tickets can be purchased at Pier 41 and Pier 43½. The **Oakland/Alameda Ferry** operates seven days a week between Alameda's Main St. Ferry Building and San Francisco's Pier 39 and the Ferry Building; tickets may be purchased on board.

FERRY LINES➤ **Golden Gate Ferry** (☎ 415/923–2000). **The Red and White Fleet** (☎ 415/546–2628). **Oakland/Alameda Ferry** (☎ 510/522–3300).

GAY & LESBIAN TRAVEL

LOCAL RESOURCES➤ The biweekly *San Francisco Bay Times* and weekly *Bay Area Reporter* are free newspapers with extensive community and entertainment listings.

INSURANCE

Travel insurance is the best way to **protect yourself against financial loss.** The most useful policies are trip-cancellation-and-interruption, default, medical, and comprehensive insurance.

Without insurance you will lose all or most of your money if you cancel your trip, regardless of the reason. It's essential that you **buy trip-cancellation-and-interruption insurance,** particularly if your airline ticket or package tour is nonrefundable and cannot be changed. When considering how much coverage you need, look for a policy that will cover the cost of your trip plus the nondiscounted price of a one-way airline ticket, should you need to return home early. Also **consider default or bankruptcy insurance,** which protects you against a supplier's failure to deliver.

Citizens of the United Kingdom can buy an annual travel-insurance policy valid for most vacations during the year in which it's purchased. If you are pregnant or have a preexisting medical condition, make sure you're covered. According to the Association of British Insurers, a trade association representing 450 insurance companies, it's wise to buy extra medical coverage when you visit the United States.

If you have purchased an expensive vacation, comprehensive insurance is a must. **Look for comprehensive policies that include trip-delay insurance,** which will protect you in the event that weather problems cause you to miss your flight, tour, or cruise. A few insurers sell waivers for preexisting medical conditions. Companies that offer both features include Access America, Carefree Travel, Travel Insured International, and Travel Guard (☞ *below*).

Always **buy travel insurance directly from the insurance company;** if you buy it from a travel agency or tour operator that goes out of business you probably will not be covered for the agency or operator's default, a major risk. Before you make any purchase, **review your existing health and homeowner's policies** to find out whether they cover expenses incurred while traveling.

TRAVEL INSURERS➤ In the U.S., **Access America** (✉ 6600 W. Broad St., Richmond, VA 23230, ☎ 804/285–3300 or 800/284–8300), **Carefree Travel Insurance** (✉ Box 9366, 100 Garden City Plaza, Garden City, NY 11530, ☎ 516/294–0220 or 800/323–3149), **Near Travel Services** (✉ Box 1339, Calumet City, IL 60409, ☎ 708/868–6700 or 800/654–6700), **Travel Guard International** (✉ 1145 Clark St., Stevens Point, WI 54481, ☎ 715/345–0505 or 800/826–1300), **Travel Insured International** (✉ Box 280568, East Hartford, CT 06128–0568, ☎ 860/528–7663 or 800/243–3174), **Travelex Insurance Services** (✉ 11717 Burt St., Suite 202, Omaha, NE 68154–1500, ☎ 402/445–8637 or 800/228–9792, FAX 800/867–9531), **Wallach & Company** (✉ 107 W. Federal St., Box 480, Middleburg, VA 20118, ☎ 540/687–3166 or 800/237–6615). In Canada, **Mutual of Omaha** (✉ Travel Division, 500 University Ave., Toronto, Ontario M5G 1V8, ☎ 416/598–4083, 800/268–8825 in Canada). In the U.K., **Association of British Insurers** (✉ 51 Gresham St., London EC2V 7HQ, ☎ 0171/600–3333).

MONEY

ATMS
Before leaving home, **make sure that your credit cards have been programmed for ATM use.**

ATM LOCATIONS➤ **Cirrus** (☎ 800/424–7787). **Plus** (☎ 800/843–7587).

MUNI
MUNI is San Francisco's transportation system of cable cars, buses, trolleys, and street cars (☞ Bus Travel, *above*).

PASSPORTS & VISAS

CANADIANS
A passport is not required to enter the United States.

U.K. CITIZENS
British citizens need a valid passport to enter the United States. If you are staying for fewer than 90 days on vacation, with a return or onward ticket, you probably will not need a visa. However, you will need to fill out the Visa Waiver Form, 1-94W, supplied by the airline.

INFORMATION➤ **London Passport Office** (☎ 0990/21010) for fees and documentation requirements and to request an emergency passport. **U.S. Embassy Visa Information Line** (☎ 01891/200290) for U.S. visa information; calls cost 49p per minute or 39p per minute cheap rate. **U.S. Embassy Visa Branch** (✉ 5 Upper Grosvenor St., London W1A 2JB) for U.S. visa information; send a self-addressed, stamped envelope. Write the **U.S. Consulate General** (✉ Queen's House, Queen St., Belfast BTI 6EO) if you live in Northern Ireland.

SENIOR-CITIZEN TRAVEL
To qualify for age-related discounts, **mention your senior-citizen status up front** when booking hotel reservations (not when

checking out) and before you're seated in restaurants (not when paying the bill). Note that discounts may be limited to certain menus, days, or hours. When renting a car, **ask about promotional car-rental discounts,** which can be cheaper than senior-citizen rates.

EDUCATIONAL TRAVEL PROGRAMS➤ **Elderhostel** (✉ 75 Federal St., 3rd floor, Boston, MA 02110, ☎ 617/ 426–7788).

SIGHTSEEING

In addition to bus and van tours of the city, most tour companies run excursions to various Bay Area and Northern California destinations such as Marin County and the Wine Country, as well as farther flung areas such as Monterey and Yosemite. City tours generally last 3½ hours and cost $25–$30.

TOUR COMPANIES➤ **Golden Gate Tours** (☎ 415/788–5775). **Gray Line-Cable Car Tours** (☎ 415/ 558–7300). **Gray Line** (☎ 415/ 558–9400). **Great Pacific Tour** (☎ 415/626–4499). **Tower Tours** (☎ 415/434–8687).

WALKING TOURS

Tours of various San Francisco neighborhoods generally cost $15–$35. Some tours have culinary themes: Lunch and snacks are often included. Trevor Hailey leads a tour focusing on the history and development of the city's gay and lesbian community. Cookbook author Shirley Fong-Torres leads a tour through Chinatown with

stops at Chinese markets and a fortune-cookie factory. The Chinese Cultural Heritage Foundation leads a Chinatown history walk and a culinary walk for groups of six or more only. City Guides, a free service sponsored by sponsored by the San Francisco Public Library, offers the greatest variety of walks, covering Chinatown, North Beach, Coit Tower, Pacific Heights mansions, Japantown, the Haight-Ashbury, historic Market Street, the Palace Hotel, and downtown roof gardens and atriums. Schedules are available at the San Francisco Visitors Center at Powell and Market streets and at library branches. Javawalk explores the history of coffee while visiting a few of San Francisco's more than 400 cafés. Victorian Home Walk is an amble through some of the city's less traveled neighborhoods: The Western Addition, Pacific Heights, and Cow Hollow.

TOUR OPERATORS➤ **Trevor Hailey** (☎ 415/550–8110). **Chinatown with the "Wok Wiz"** (☎ 650/ 355–9657). **Chinese Cultural Heritage Foundation** (☎ 415/986– 1822). **City Guides** (☎ 415/ 557–4266). **Javawalk** (☎ 415/ 673–9255). **Victorian Home Walk** (☎ 415/252–9485).

STUDENTS

To save money, **look into deals available through student-oriented travel agencies.** To qualify you'll need a bona fide student ID card.

Members of international student groups are also eligible.

STUDENT IDs AND SERVICES➤ **Council on International Educational Exchange** (⊠ CIEE, 205 E. 42nd St., 14th floor, New York, NY 10017, ☎ 212/822–2600 or 888/268–6245, FAX 212/822–2699), for mail orders only, in the United States. **Travel Cuts** (⊠ 187 College St., Toronto, Ontario M5T 1P7, ☎ 416/979–2406 or 800/667–2887) in Canada.

TELEPHONES

In 1997 the 415 area code split off so that numbers in the Peninsula south of San Francisco use 650.

CALLING HOME

AT&T, MCI, and Sprint long-distance services make calling home relatively convenient and let you avoid hotel surcharges. Typically you dial an 800 number in the United States.

TO OBTAIN ACCESS CODES➤ **AT&T USADirect** (☎ 800/874–4000). **MCI Call USA** (☎ 800/444–4444). **Sprint Express** (☎ 800/793–1153).

TOUR OPERATORS

Buying a prepackaged tour or independent vacation can make your trip to San Francisco less expensive and more hassle-free. Because everything is prearranged you'll spend less time planning.

Operators that handle several hundred thousand travelers per year can use their purchasing power to give you a good price. Their high volume may also indicate financial stability. But some small companies provide more personalized service; because they tend to specialize, they may also be more knowledgeable about a given area.

A GOOD DEAL?

The more your package or tour includes, the better you can predict the ultimate cost of your vacation. Make sure you know exactly what is covered, and **beware of hidden costs.** Are taxes, tips, and service charges included? Transfers and baggage handling? Entertainment and excursions? These can add up.

If the package or tour you are considering is priced lower than in your wildest dreams, **be skeptical.** Also, **make sure your travel agent knows the accommodations** and other services. Ask about the hotel's location, room size, beds, and whether it has a pool, room service, or programs for children, if you care about these. Has your agent been there in person or sent others you can contact?

BUYER BEWARE

Each year consumers are stranded or lose their money when tour operators—even very large ones with excellent reputations—go out of business. So **check out the operator.** Find out how long the company has been in business, and ask several agents about its reputation. **Don't book unless the firm has a consumer-protection program.**

Members of the National Tour Association and United States Tour Operators Association are required to set aside funds to cover your payments and travel arrangements in case the company defaults. Nonmembers may carry insurance instead. Look for the details, and for the name of an underwriter with a solid reputation, in the operator's brochure. Note: When it comes to tour operators, **don't trust escrow accounts.** Although the Department of Transportation watches over charter-flight operators, no regulatory body prevents tour operators from raiding the till. You may want to protect yourself by buying travel insurance that includes a tour-operator default provision. For more information, *see* Consumer Protection, *above*.

It's also a good idea to choose a company that participates in the American Society of Travel Agent's Tour Operator Program (TOP). This gives you a forum if there are any disputes between you and your tour operator; ASTA will act as mediator.

Tour-Operator Recommendations➤ **National Tour Association** (✉ NTA, 546 E. Main St., Lexington, KY 40508, ☎ 606/226–4444 or 800/755–8687). **United States Tour Operators Association** (✉ USTOA, 342 Madison Ave., Suite 1522, New York,

NY 10173, ☎ 212/599–6599, FAX 212/599–6744). **American Society of Travel Agents** (☞ *below*).

USING AN AGENT

Travel agents are excellent resources. In fact, large operators accept bookings made only through travel agents. But it's a good idea to **collect brochures from several agencies,** because some agents' suggestions may be influenced by relationships with tour and package firms that reward them for volume sales. If you have a special interest, **find an agent with expertise in that area;** ASTA (☞ Travel Agencies, *below*) has a database of specialists worldwide. Do some homework on your own, too: Local tourism boards can provide information about lesser-know and small-niche operators, some of which may sell only direct.

PACKAGES

Like group tours, independent vacation packages are available from major tour operators and airlines. The companies listed below offer vacation packages in a broad price range.

Air/Hotel/Car➤ **American Airlines Fly AAway Vacations** (☎ 800/321–2121). **Continental Vacations** (☎ 800/634–5555). **Delta Dream Vacations** (☎ 800/872–7786). **United Vacations** (☎ 800/328–6877). **US Airways Vacations** (☎ 800/455–0123).

HOTEL ONLY➤ SuperCities (✉ 139 Main St., Cambridge, MA 02142, ☎ 800/333–1234).

CUSTOM PACKAGES➤ **Amtrak's Great American Vacations** (☎ 800/321–8684). Also contact **Budget WorldClass Drive** (☎ 800/527–0700, 0800/181181 in the U.K.) for self-drive itineraries.

FROM THE U.K.➤ Tour operators offering packages to San Francisco include **British Airways Holidays** (✉ Astral Towers, Betts Way, London Rd., Crawley, West Sussex RH10 2XA, ☎ 01293/723121), **Jetsave** (✉ Sussex House, London Rd., East Grinstead, West Sussex RH19 1LD, ☎ 01342/312033), **Key to America** (✉ 1–3 Station Rd., Ashford, Middlesex TW15 2UW, ☎ 01784/248777), **Kuoni Travel Ltd.** (✉ Kuoni House, Dorking, Surrey RH5 4AZ, ☎ 01306/742222), **Premier Holidays** (✉ Premier Travel Center, Westbrook, Milton Rd., Cambridge CB4 1YG, ☎ 01223/516688), and **Trailfinders** (✉ 42–50 Earls Court Rd., London W8 6FT, ☎ 0171/937–5400; ✉ 58 Deansgate, Manchester, M3 2FF, ☎ 0161/839–6969).

TRAVEL AGENCIES

A good travel agent puts your needs first. Look for an agency that has been in business at least five years, emphasizes customer service, and has someone on staff who specializes in your destination. In addition, **make sure the agency belongs to the American Society of Travel Agents** (ASTA). If your travel agency is also acting as your tour operator, *see* Tour Operators, *above*.

LOCAL AGENT REFERRALS➤ **American Society of Travel Agents** (ASTA, ☎ 800/965–2782 24-hr hot line, FAX 703/684–8319). **Alliance of Canadian Travel Associations** (✉ Suite 201, 1729 Bank St., Ottawa, Ontario K1V 7Z5, ☎ 613/521–0474, FAX 613/521–0805). **Association of British Travel Agents** (✉ 55–57 Newman St., London W1P 4AH, ☎ 0171/637–2444, FAX 0171/637–0713).

VISITOR INFORMATION

CITY➤ **San Francisco Convention and Visitors Bureau** (✉ 201 3rd St., Suite 900, 94103–3185, ☎ 415/974–6900).

STATE➤ **California Office of Tourism** (✉ 801 K St., Suite 1600, Sacramento, CA 95814, ☎ 916/322–2882 or 800/862–2543) has a free visitor's guide.

IN THE U.K.➤ **California Tourist Office** (✉ ABC California, Box 35, Abingdon, Oxfordshire OX14 4TB, ☎ 0891/200278). Calls cost 50p per minute peak rate or 45p per minute cheap rate. For a brochure send a check for £3 payable to ABC California at the above address.

WHEN TO GO

You can **visit San Francisco comfortably any time of year;** the climate always feels Mediterranean and moderate—albeit with a foggy, sometimes chilly twist. The temperature rarely drops lower than 40°F, and anything warmer than 80°F is considered a heat wave. Be prepared for rain in winter, especially December and January. Winds off the ocean can add to the chill factor, so pack warm clothing. North, east, and south of the city, summers are warmer.

CLIMATE

FORECASTS➤ **Weather Channel Connection** (☎ 900/932–8437), 95¢ per minute from a Touch-Tone phone. In San Francisco, recorded information is available free through the **National Weather Service's San Francisco Bay Area office** (☎ 415/936–1212).

The following chart lists the average daily maximum and minimum temperatures for San Francisco.

Climate in San Francisco

Jan.	56F	13C	May	64F	17C	Sept.	70F	21C
	46F	8C		51F	10C		56F	13C
Feb.	60F	15C	June	66F	19C	Oct.	69F	20C
	48F	9C		53F	11C		55F	13C
Mar.	61F	16C	July	66F	19C	Nov.	64F	18C
	49F	9C		54F	12C		51F	10C
Apr.	63F	17C	Aug.	66F	19C	Dec.	57F	14C
	50F	10C		54F	12C		47F	8C

1 Destination: San Francisco

SPLENDOR IN THE FOG

THAT VISITORS WILL ENVY San Franciscans is a given—at least, so say Bay Area residents, who tend to pity anyone who did not have the fortune to settle here. (There's probably never been a time when the majority of the population was native born.) Their self-satisfaction may surprise some, considering how the city has been battered by fires and earthquakes from the 1840s onward, most notably in the 1906 conflagration and in 1989, when the Loma Prieta earthquake, rocked the city's foundations once more. Since its earliest days San Francisco has been a phoenix, the mythical bird that periodically dies in flame to be reborn in greater grandeur.

Its latest rebirth has occurred in SoMa, the neighborhood south of Market Street, where the Yerba Buena Gardens development has taken shape with the world-class SFMOMA (San Francisco Museum of Modern Art) at its heart—transforming a formerly seedy neighborhood into a magnet of culture. As a peninsula city, surrounded on three sides by water, San Francisco grows from the inside out; its blighted areas are improved, not abandoned. The museum development's instant success—measured by a huge influx of residents, suburban commuters, and international visitors—perfectly exemplifies a long tradition of starting from scratch to rebuild and improve.

In its first life San Francisco was little more than a small, well-situated settlement. Founded by Spaniards in 1776, it was prized for its natural harbor, so commodious that "all the navies of the world might fit inside it," as one visitor wrote. Around 1849 the discovery of gold at John Sutter's sawmill in the nearby Sierra foothills transformed the sleepy little settlement into a city of 30,000. Millions of dollars' worth of gold was panned and blasted out of the hills, the impetus for the development of a western Wall Street. Fueled by the 1859 discovery of a fabulously rich vein of silver in Virginia City, Nevada, the population soared to 342,000. In 1869 the transcontinental railway was completed, linking the once-isolated western capital to the East; San Francisco had become a major city of the United States.

The boom was not without its prices; the hardships of immigrant railroad workers led to a strong tradition of feisty labor unions.

And contentiousness is still part of the price San Francisco pays for variety. Consider the makeup of the city's chief administrative body, the 11-member Board of Supervisors: Chinese, Hispanics, gays, blacks, and women have all been representatives. The city is a bastion of what it likes to refer to as progressive politics. The Sierra Club, founded here in 1892 by John Muir, who was its first president, has its national headquarters on Polk Street. The turn-of-the-century "yellow journalism" of William Randolph Hearst's *San Francisco Examiner* gave way to leftish publications such as *Mother Jones* magazine and today's daily newspapers. Political bitterness has sometimes led to violence, most spectacularly Bloody Thursday, the face-off between striking longshoremen and scab labor in 1934, and the 1978 assassinations of the city's liberal mayor, George Moscone, and its first gay supervisor, Harvey Milk, by a vindictive right-wing ex-supervisor. However, despite a boomtown tendency toward raucousness and a sad history of anti-Asian discrimination, the city today prides itself on its tolerance. The mix, everybody knows, is what makes San Francisco. On any given night at the Opera House—a major civic crossroads—you can see costumes ranging from torn denim and full leather to business suits, dinner jackets, and sequined, feathered gowns—not to mention the occasional goodwill-store find on a well-dressed drag queen.

LOOSE, TOLERANT, AND even licentious are words that are used to describe San Francisco; bohemian communities thrive here. As early as the 1860s the Barbary Coast—a collection of taverns, whorehouses, and gambling joints along Pacific Avenue close to the waterfront—was famous, or infamous. North Beach, the city's Little Italy, became the home of the beat movement in the 1950s (Herb Caen, the city's best-known columnist, coined the term beatnik). Lawrence Ferlinghetti's City Lights, a bookstore and publishing house that still stands on Columbus Avenue brought out, among other titles, Allen Ginsberg's *Howl* and *Kaddish*. Across Broadway a plaque identifies the Condor as the site of the nation's first topless and bottomless performances, a monument to a slightly later era. In the '60s the Free Speech Movement began at the University of California at Berkeley, and Stanford's David Harris, who went to prison for defying the draft, numbered among the nation's most famous student leaders. In October 1965 Allen Ginsberg introduced the term *flower power,* and the Haight-Ashbury district became synonymous with hippiedom, giving rise to such legendary bands as Jefferson Airplane, Big Brother and the Holding Company (fronted by Janis Joplin), and the Grateful Dead. Thirty years later the Haight's history and its name still draw neo-hippies, as well as new wavers with black lips and blue hair, and some rather menacing skinheads. Transients who now sleep in nearby Golden Gate Park make panhandling one of Haight Street's major business activities, and the potential for crime and violence after dark has turned many of the liberal residents into unlikely law-and-order advocates who organize neighborhood patrols to watch for trouble. Still, most remain committed to keeping the Haight the Haight.

SOUTHWEST OF THE Haight is the onetime Irish neighborhood known as the Castro, which during the 1970s became identified with gay and lesbian liberation. Castro Street is dominated by the elaborate Castro Theatre, a 1922 vision in Spanish baroque style, which presents first-run art and independent films with occasional revivals of Hollywood film classics. (The grand old pipe organ still plays during intermissions, breaking into "San Francisco" just before the feature begins.) There's been much talk, most of it exaggerated, about how AIDS has "chastened" and "matured" the Castro. The disease *has* spawned the creation of AIDS education, treatment, and care-giving networks, such as Shanti and Open Hand, models for the rest of the nation. The Castro is still an effervescent neighborhood, and has become relatively upscale. It's also an increasingly mixed area and gays now reside in neighborhoods all around the city.

In terms of both geography and culture, San Francisco is about as close as you can get to Asia in the continental United States. (The city prides itself on its role as a Pacific Rim capital, and overseas investment has become a vital part of its financial life.) The first great wave of Chinese immigrants came as railroad laborers. Chinese workers quickly became the target of racial hatred and discriminatory laws; Chinatown—which began when the Chinese moved into old buildings that white businesses seeking more fashionable locations had abandoned—developed as a refuge, as much as anything else. It is still a fascinating place to wander and a good bet for late-night food, but it's not the whole story by any means. The Asian community, which now accounts for a fifth of San Francisco's population, reaches into every San Francisco neighborhood and particularly into the Sunset and Richmond districts, west toward the ocean. Clement Street, which runs through the center of the Richmond District, has become the main thoroughfare of a second Chinatown. Southeast Asian immigrants, many of them ethnic Chinese, are transforming the seedy Tenderloin into a thriving Little Indochina. There was heavy Japanese immigration earlier in this century, but most of it went to southern California, where organized labor had less of a foothold and where there were greater opportunities for Asian workers. Still, San Francisco has its Japantown, with the Japan Center complex and a handful of shops and restaurants. Working hard to establish themselves over the decades, today Asian-Americans of every persuasion are at the highest levels of the city's elected and appointed government and in leadership positions in San Francisco's business, medical, and educational communities.

GEOGRAPHICALLY, San Francisco is the thumbnail on a 40-mi thumb of land, the San Francisco Peninsula, which stretches northward between the Pacific Ocean and San Francisco Bay. Hemmed in on three sides by water, its land area (less than 50 square mi) is relatively small; the population, at about 750,000, is small, too. Technically speaking, it's only California's fourth-largest city, behind Los Angeles, San Diego, and nearby San Jose. But that statistic is misleading: The

Bay Area, which stretches from the bedroom communities north of Oakland and Berkeley south through the peninsula and the San Jose area, is really one continuous megacity, with San Francisco as its heart.

Not so many centuries ago the area that was to become San Francisco was a windswept, virtually treeless, and, above all, sandy wasteland. Sand even covered the hills. The sand is still there, but—except along the ocean—it's well hidden. City hall is built on 80 ft of it. The westerly section of the city—the Sunset and Richmond districts and Golden Gate Park—seems flat only because sand has filled in the contours of the hills.

But the hills that remain are spectacular. They provide vistas all over the city—nothing is more common than to find yourself staring out toward Angel Island or Alcatraz, or across the bay at Berkeley and Oakland. The hills also made cable cars a necessity early on. The city's two bridges, which are almost as majestic as their surroundings, had their 50th birthdays in 1986 and 1987. The Golden Gate Bridge, which crosses to Marin County, got a bigger party, but the San Francisco–Oakland Bay Bridge got a better present: a necklace of lights along its spans. They were supposed to be temporary, but the locals were so taken with the glimmer that bridge boosters started a drive to make them permanent; radio DJs and newspaper columnists put out daily appeals, drivers gave extra quarters to the toll takers, various corporations put up shares, and now—nearly one million dollars later—the lights on the Bay Bridge shine nightly.

FIRST-TIME VISITORS to San Francisco sometimes arrive with ideas about its weather gleaned from movie images of sunny California or from a misinformed 1967 song that celebrated "a warm San Franciscan night." Sunny, perhaps; warm—not likely. That's *southern* California. (A perennially popular T-shirt quotes Mark Twain's alleged remark: "The coldest winter I ever spent was a summer in San Francisco.") Still, it almost never freezes here, and heat waves are equally rare. Most San Franciscans come to love the climate, which is genuinely temperate— sufficiently welcoming for the imposing row of palms down the median of Dolores Street but seldom warm enough for just a T-shirt at night. The coastal stretch of ocean may look inviting, but the surfers you sometimes see along Ocean Beach are wearing wet suits (though the beach can be fine for sunning). And, of course, there's the famous fog— something that tourists tend to find more delightful than do the residents. It's largely a summer phenomenon; San Francisco's real summer begins in September, when the fog lifts and the air warms up for a while. November brings on the rains.

Victorian architecture is as integral to the city as fog and cable cars. Bay-windowed, ornately decorated Victorian houses—the ahistorical, multicolor paint jobs that have become popular make them seem even more ornate—are the city's most distinguishing architectural feature. They date mainly from the latter part of Queen Victoria's reign, 1870 to the turn of the century. In those three decades San Francisco more than doubled in population (from 150,000 to 342,000); the transcontinental railway, linking the once-isolated western capital to the East, had been completed in 1869. That may explain the exuberant confidence of the architecture.

Over the years plenty of the Victorians have gone under the wrecker's ball to make way for such commercial projects as shopping complexes or for the low-income housing projects that went up under the rubric of "urban renewal" but quickly degenerated into slums. The decrepit old houses were out of favor for a while, but once the era of gentrification arrived, those still standing were snatched up, fixed up, and sold at exorbitant prices. So parts of the city that not so long ago were considered ghettos are becoming expensive places to live.

But higher prices in no way deter the hordes from flocking to the City by the Bay. In addition to a skyrocketing population, visitors keep coming for events throughout the year. The Gay and Lesbian Freedom Day Parade, held each June, vies with the Chinese New Year's Parade, an annual February event, as the city's most elaborate. They both get competition from Japantown's Cherry Blossom Festival, in April; the Columbus Day and St. Patrick's Day parades; Carnaval, held in the Hispanic Mission District in May; and the May Day march, a labor celebration in a labor town. The mix of ethnic, economic, social, and sexual groups can be bewildering, but the city's residents—whatever their origin—face it with aplomb and even gratitude. Everybody in San Francisco has an opinion about where to get the best burrito or the hottest Szechuan eggplant or the strongest cappuccino, and even the most staid citizens have learned to appreciate the cleverly campy. Nearly everyone smiles on the fortunate day they arrived on this windy, foggy patch of peninsula.

2 Exploring San Francisco

By Toni Chapman

Updated by Vincent Bielski

YOU COULD LIVE IN SAN FRANCISCO a month and ask no greater entertainment than walking through it," waxed Inez Hayes Irwin, the author of *The Californiacs,* an effusive 1921 homage to the state of California and the City by the Bay. Her claim remains as true as ever today: As in the '20s, touring on foot is the best way to experience this diverse metropolis.

San Francisco is a relatively small city, with just over 750,000 residents nested on a 46½-square-mi tip of land between San Francisco Bay and the Pacific Ocean. San Franciscans cherish the city's colorful past, and many older buildings have been spared from demolition and nostalgically converted into modern offices and shops. Longtime locals rue the sites that got away—spectacular railroad and mining-boom-era residences lost in the 1906 earthquake, the elegant Fox Theater, and Playland at the Beach. But despite acts of God, the indifference of developers, and the mixed record of the city's planning commission, much of the architectural and historical interest remains. Bernard Maybeck, Julia Morgan, Willis Polk, and Arthur Brown Jr. are among the noted architects whose designs still remain in the city's downtown and in its neighborhoods.

San Francisco's charms are great and small. First-time visitors won't want to miss Golden Gate Park, the Palace of Fine Arts, the Golden Gate Bridge, or a cable car ride on Nob Hill. But a walk down the Filbert Steps or through Macondray Lane, or a peaceful hour gazing east from Ina Coolbrith Park can be equally inspiring.

San Francisco neighborhoods are self-aware, and they retain strong cultural, political, and ethnic identities. Locals know this pluralism is the real life of the city. Experiencing San Francisco means visiting the neighborhoods: the colorful Mission District, gay Castro, countercultural Haight Street, serene Pacific Heights, bustling Chinatown, and still-bohemian North Beach.

Exploring involves navigating a maze of one-way streets and restricted parking zones. Public parking garages or lots tend to be expensive, as are hotel parking spaces. San Francisco's famed 40-plus hills can be a problem for drivers who are new to the terrain. Cable cars, buses, trolleys, and Metro streetcars, which run underground along Market Street, can take you to or near many of the area's attractions.

Union Square

Although the rest of the city feels like a collection of small towns strung together, Union Square (and the adjacent downtown area) bustles with big-city bravado. Since 1850 Union Square has been the heart of San Francisco's downtown. Its name derives from a series of violent pro-union demonstrations staged here just prior to the Civil War. This is where you will find the city's finest department stores, its most exclusive boutiques, and its leading art galleries. Among the galleries are John Berggruen on Grant Avenue, Meyerovich on Post Street, and the Fraenkel and Robert Koch galleries on Geary.

The square itself is a 2½-acre oasis planted with palms, boxwood, and seasonal flowers and peopled with a kaleidoscope of characters: office workers, street musicians, several very vocal preachers, and a fair share of homeless people. Throughout the year the square hosts numerous public events: fashion shows, free noontime concerts, ethnic celebrations, and noisy demonstrations. Auto and bus traffic is often gridlocked on the four streets bordering the square. Post, Stockton, and Geary streets are one-way, while Powell runs in both directions until it crosses Geary, where it becomes one-way to Market Street. Union Square covers a convenient but costly four-story underground garage; approximately 3,000 cars are parked here on busy days. For cheaper parking try the nearby Sutter-Stockton Garage.

Numbers in the text margin correspond to numbers in the margin and on the Downtown San Francisco map.

Sights to See

② Cable car terminus. This is the starting point for two of the three operating lines. The Powell-Mason line climbs up Nob Hill, then winds through North Beach to Fisherman's Wharf. The Powell-Hyde car also crosses Nob Hill but then continues up Russian Hill and down Hyde Street to Victorian Park, across from the Buena Vista Cafe and near Ghirardelli Square. The cable car system dates from 1873, when Andrew Hallidie demonstrated his first car on Clay Street; in 1964 the tramlike vehicles were designated National Historic landmarks. Before 1900, 500 cable cars spanned a network of 110 mi. Today there are 45 cars on three lines, and the network covers just 10 mi. Most of the cars date from the last century, although the cars and lines had a complete $58 million overhaul during the early 1980s. In summertime there are often long lines to board any of the three systems. Buy your ticket ($2 one-way) on board, at nearby hotels, or at the police/information booth near the turnaround (☞ Cable Cars *in* Essential Information).

The panhandlers, street preachers, and other regulars at this terminus can be daunting. A pleasant alternative is to stand in line at the Hyde Street end of the Powell-Hyde line, which affords views of the bay and Golden Gate Bridge (☞ The Northern Waterfront, *below*). Better yet, if it's just the experience of riding a cable car you're after (rather than a trip to the wharf or Nob Hill), board the less-busy California line at Van Ness Avenue and ride it down to the Hyatt Regency (☞ Chapter 4). ⊠ *Powell and Market Sts.*

450 Sutter Street. This 1928 terra-cotta skyscraper (now a medical and dental office) is an art deco masterpiece, with handsome Mayan-inspired designs covering both the exterior and interior surfaces. ⊠ *Between Stockton and Powell Sts.*

❼ Hallidie Building. View this building, named for cable car inventor Andrew Hallidie, from across the street. Willis Polk's revolutionary glass-curtain wall—believed to be the world's first such structure—hangs a foot beyond the reinforced concrete of the frame. With its reflecting glass, decorative exterior fire escapes that appear to be metal balconies, and Venetian Gothic cornice, the unusual building dominates the block. Also notice the horizontal ornamental bands of birds at feeders. ⊠ *130 Sutter St., between Kearny and Montgomery Sts.*

❻ Hammersmith Building. Glass walls and a playful design distinguish this small, colorful beaux arts–style structure, built in 1907. The Foundation for Architectural Heritage once described the building as a "commercial jewel box"; ap-

12

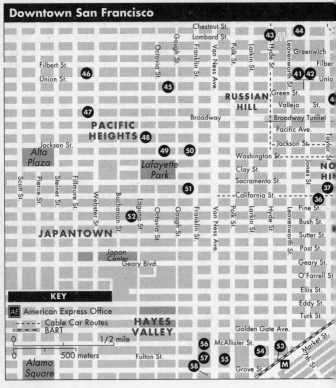

Downtown San Francisco

KEY

AE American Express Office

----- Cable Car Routes

━━━ BART

0 .... 1/2 mile

0 .... 500 meters

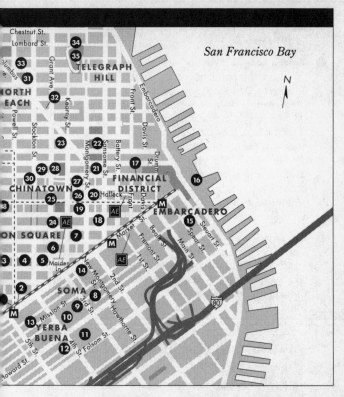

propriately, it was originally designed for use as a jewelry store. Buy breakfast downstairs at **Franciscan Croissants.** ✉ *301 Sutter St.*

⑤ Maiden Lane. Known as Morton Street in the Barbary Coast era, this red-light district reported at least one murder a week. After the 1906 fire destroyed the brothels, the street emerged as Maiden Lane, and it has since become a chic, daytime pedestrian mall, with a patchwork of umbrella-shaded tables, between Stockton and Kearny streets. The brick structure at **140 Maiden Lane** (☎ 415/989–2100) is the only Frank Lloyd Wright structure in San Francisco. With its circular interior ramp and skylights, it is said to have been a model for the Guggenheim Museum in New York. It now houses the Circle Gallery, which shows the limited-edition art jewelry (worth a look) of Erté.

① San Francisco Visitors Information Center. Conveniently located below the cable car terminus, the center is open daily (except holidays), and the multilingual staff will answer specific questions as well as provide maps, brochures, and information on daily events. Visitors can pick up coupons for substantial savings on tourist attractions as well as pamphlets (and depending on the season, discount vouchers) for most downtown hotels. ✉ *Hallidie Plaza, lower level, Powell and Market Sts.,* ☎ *415/391–2000.* ☉ *Weekdays 9–5:30, Sat. 9–3, Sun. 10–2.*

TIX Bay Area. This excellent service provides half-price day-of-performance tickets (cash or traveler's checks only) to all types of performing arts events, as well as regular full-price box office services for concerts, clubs, and sporting events (credit cards accepted). Telephone reservations are not accepted for half-price tickets. Also available are Explorer Passes, which provide entry to Golden Gate Park's museums at a discount rate, and Muni Passports, short-term tourist passes for all city buses and cable cars. ✉ *Stockton St. at Union Square,* ☎ *415/433–7827.* ☉ *Tues.–Thurs. 11–6, Fri.–Sat. 11–7.*

④ Union Square. At center stage, the *Victory Monument,* by Robert Ingersoll Aitken, commemorates Commodore George Dewey's victory over the Spanish fleet at Manila in 1898. The 97-ft Corinthian column, topped by a bronze figure symbolizing naval conquest, was dedicated by Theodore Roosevelt in 1903 and withstood the 1906 earthquake. After the earthquake and fire of 1906, the square was dubbed "Little St. Francis" because of the temporary shelter erected for residents of the St. Francis Hotel. Actor John Barrymore was among the guests pressed into volunteering to stack bricks in the square. ⊠ *Between Powell, Stockton, Post, and Geary Sts.*

❸ **Westin St. Francis Hotel.** The second-oldest hotel in the city, originally built in 1904, was conceived by Charles Crocker and his associates as an elegant hostelry for their millionaire friends. Swift service and sumptuous surroundings—glass chandeliers, a gilt ceiling, and marble columns—are hallmarks of the property. A sybarite's dream, the hotel's Turkish baths once had ocean water piped in. After the hotel was ravaged by the 1906 quake, a new, larger, more luxurious residence was opened in 1907. In 1975 Sara Jane Moore, standing among a crowd outside the hotel, attempted to shoot then-president Gerald Ford. No plaques commemorate this event in the establishment's lobby. The ever-helpful staff will, however, gladly direct you to the traditional teatime ritual, held daily from 3 to 5 or if you prefer, to champagne and caviar in the dramatic art deco **Compass Rose** lounge (☎ 415/774–0167). Elaborate Chinese screens, secluded seating alcoves, and soothing background music make this an ideal rest stop. Reservations for the lounge are not required, but walk-ins should expect a wait during December and on weekends. ⊠ *335 Powell St., at Geary St.,* ☎ *415/397–7000.*

South of Market (SoMa) and the Embarcadero

The vast tract of downtown land south of Market Street along the waterfront and west to the Mission District—also known by the acronym SoMa (inspired by New York City's south-of-Houston SoHo)—has recently become the center of a burgeoning arts scene and, for the first time, a major destination. This is big news in a one-time industrial neighborhood that was once the stomping ground of alternative artists and the gay leather set. At the heart of the action are the San Francisco Museum of Modern Art (SFMOMA), now the city's most popular museum, and the Center for the Arts at Yerba Buena Gardens, which hosts some of the most ambitious, multi-ethnic work in the city.

The mood is upscale industrial, especially around the new arts centers and in many of the trendy restaurants. The gentrifying South Park area is where the cybercrowd from *Wired* magazine and other new media tank up on lattes and toasted baguettes. Yet even with the influx of money, the neighborhood still has an edge that keeps it interesting.

Sights to See

⑫ **Ansel Adams Center for Photography.** Ansel Adams himself created this center in Carmel in 1967. In 1989 it moved to SoMa, where it became the first arts organization built at the new Yerba Buena Center complex. The center showcases a wonderful variety of historical and contemporary photography as well as changing exhibitions of Adams's work. ⊠ *250 4th St.,* ☎ *415/495–7000.* ▨ *$5.* ☉ *Tues.–Sun. 11–5, 1st Thurs. of month 11–8.*

California Historical Society. Founded in 1871, this vast repository of Californiana contains 500,000 photographs, 150,000 manuscripts, thousands of books, periodicals, prints, and paintings as well as gold rush paraphernalia. The new building is an airy, sky-lit space with a central gallery, two adjacent galleries, a research library, and a storefront bookstore. ⊠ *678 Mission St.,* ☎ *415/357–1848.* ▨ *$3.* ☉ *Tues.–Sat. 11–5.*

⑬ **Cartoon Art Museum.** Krazy Kat, Zippy the Pinhead, Batman, and a whole crew of other colorful cartoon icons greet you as you walk in the door to the Cartoon Art Museum. In addition to a 11,000-piece permanent collection, a 3,000-volume library, and a CD-ROM gallery, there are meticulously curated changing exhibits covering everything from the impact of underground comics to female cartoonists, the *Peanuts'* 45th anniversary, and African-American cartoonists. The museum store is excellent. ⊠ *814 Mission St., Suite 200,* ☎ *415/546–3922.* ▨ *$4.* ☉ *Wed.–Fri. 11–5, Sat. 10–5, Sun. 1–5.*

⑨ **Center for the Arts.** Within the Yerba Buena Gardens complex, the center showcases dance, music, performance, theater, visual arts, film, video, and installations—from the community-based to the international—with an emphasis on the cultural diversity of San Francisco. The complex includes a theater and a forum, three visual arts galleries, a film and video screening room, a gift shop, a café, and an outdoor performance stage, where there's midday music daily from April through October. ⊠ *701 Mission St.,* ☎ *415/978–2787.* 🎟 *Galleries $5; free 1st Thurs. of month 6–8 PM.* ◔ *Galleries and box office: Tues.–Sun. 11–6.*

⑰ **Embarcadero Center.** Designed by John Portman in the late 1970s, the architectural landmark is often called "Rockefeller Center West." The complex includes more than 100 shops, 40 restaurants, and two hotels, as well as office space. Louise Nevelson's dramatic 54-ft-high black-steel sculpture, *Sky Tree,* stands guard over Building 3 and is among 20-plus nationally renowned pieces of art throughout the center (guided art tours available). The **Hyatt Regency Hotel's** spectacular lobby (featured in the 1970s disaster epic *The Towering Inferno*) has a 20-story hanging garden and glass elevators that are fun to ride. The Embarcadero recently expanded with an indoor–outdoor sky deck offering an enticing 360-degree view of the city, a World Internet Center, a holiday ice-skating rink, and a five-screen cinema showing first-run artsy and foreign films. For information on events call 800/733–6318 or 415/772–0500. ⊠ *Clay St. between Battery St. and the Embarcadero.* ◔ *Weekdays 10–7, Sat. 10–6, Sun. noon–6.*

⑯ **Ferry Building.** The beacon of the port area is the Embarcadero's quaint Ferry Building, with its 230-ft clock tower modeled after the campanile of Seville's cathedral. The building has held its post since 1896 and is now the headquarters of the Port Commission and the World Trade Center's office. A waterfront promenade that extends from the piers north of here to the San Francisco–Oakland Bay Bridge is great for jogging, in-line skating, watching sailboats on the bay, or enjoying a picnic. Ferries from behind the Ferry Building sail to Sausalito, Larkspur, Tiburon, and the East Bay. Across from the building the **Ferry Plaza Farmers' Market,** with organic produce from noted growers, is held every Saturday morning.

North of the Ferry Building is the initial section of the **Promenade Ribbon,** a narrow cement-and-glass strip that runs along the waterfront. Take a stroll on the pedestrian pier adjacent to Pier 5, with its old-fashioned lamps, wrought-iron benches, and awe-inspiring views of the bay—but beware of kamikaze skateboarders. ⊠ *The Embarcadero, between Mission and Vallejo Sts.*

The Jewish Museum. This small museum hosts revolving shows on Jewish history and culture as well as art exhibits on aspects of Jewish culture. The curators here don't shy away from controversial programs, hosting exhibits such as *Art and the Rosenberg Era*, an in-depth look at freedom of expression, and *Bridges & Boundaries: African Americans and American Jews*. The museum plans to move into the Yerba Buena Center in the year 2000. ⊠ *121 Steuart St.,* ☎ *415/543–8880.* ☒ *$5; free 1st Mon. of month.* ☉ *Mon.–Wed. noon–6, Thurs. noon–8, Sun. 11–6.*

Justin Herman Plaza. The plaza plays host to arts-and-crafts shows, street musicians, skateboarders, and mimes on weekends year-round; it's also a popular place to fly kites. A huge concrete sculpture, the **Vaillancourt Fountain,** has had legions of critics since its installation in 1971: Many feel it is an eyesore. ⊠ *The Embarcadero, north of Market St.*

Market Street buildings. Market Street, which bisects the city at an angle, has consistently challenged San Francisco's architects. One of the most intriguing responses sits diagonally across Market Street from the Palace Hotel. The tower of the **Hobart Building** (⊠ 582 Market St.) combines a flat facade and oval sides and is considered one of architect Willis Polk's best works in the city. Farther east on Market Street is another classic solution, Charles Havens's triangular **Flatiron Building** (⊠ 540–548 Market St.). Farther on, at **388 Market,** a sleek, angled building by Skidmore, Owings, and Merrill is another must-see. Holding its own against the skyscrapers that tower over this intersection is the **Donahue Monument** (⊠ Market and Battery Sts.). This homage to waterfront mechanics was designed by Douglas Tilden, a noted California sculptor who was deaf and mute. The plaque below it marks the spot as the location of the San Francisco Bay shoreline in 1848. ⊠ *Market St. between New Montgomery and Beale Sts.*

⓫ Moscone Convention Center. The site of the 1984 Democratic convention is distinguished by a contemporary glass-

and-girder lobby at street level (all convention exhibit space is underground) and a monolithic, column-free interior. ⊠ *Howard St. between 3rd and 4th Sts.*

⑭ Palace Hotel. The Palace, a Sheraton property, has resumed its place among San Francisco's grandest hotels. Opened in 1875, it is the oldest hotel in the city and boasts a storied past, some of which is recounted in glass cases off the main lobby. President Warren Harding died here while still in office in 1923. The original Palace was destroyed by fire following the 1906 earthquake despite its 28,000-gallon reservoir fed by four artesian wells. The current building dates from 1909; late-1980s renovations included the restoration of the glass-dome Garden Court restaurant and the installation of original mosaic-tile floors in Oriental-rug designs. Maxfield Parrish's wall-size painting, *The Pied Piper,* dominates the hotel's Pied Piper Bar. There are guided tours of the hotel's grand interior (☎ 415/546–5026) Tuesday, Wednesday, and Saturday at 10:30 AM and Thursday at 2 PM. ⊠ *2 New Montgomery St.,* ☎ *415/392–8600.*

⑮ Rincon Center. A stunning five-story rain column resembling a mini-rainstorm stands out as the centerpiece of the mall at this popular civic center. In addition to the mall, there are two modern towers of offices and apartments, with an old post office built in the Streamline Moderne style. In the post office's historic lobby is a series of Anton Refregier murals—one of the largest Works Projects Administration–era (WPA) art endeavors—with 27 panels depicting California life from the days when Native Americans were the state's sole inhabitants through World War I. Completion of this significant work was interrupted by World War II and political infighting; the latter led to some alteration in Refregier's "radical" historical interpretations. A permanent exhibit displays interesting photographs and artifacts of life in the Rincon area in the 1800s. Back in the mall, several new murals reflect San Francisco in the '90s—office workers at computers, sporting events, and the like. ⊠ *Between Steuart, Spear, Mission, and Howard Sts.*

San Francisco Marriott. Its 40-story ziggurat construction topped with reflecting glass pinwheels has elicited gasps from newspaper columnists and passersby, earning it comparisons with a jukebox, a high-rise parking meter, and a giant thermometer. ⊠ *4th and Mission Sts.*

★ ❽ **San Francisco Museum of Modern Art.** SFMOMA took center stage in the SoMa arts scene in January 1995, winning immediate international acclaim for its adventurous programming, which includes traveling exhibits and multimedia installations. The strong permanent collection includes works by Matisse, Picasso, O'Keeffe, Frida Kahlo, Jackson Pollock, and Warhol, as well as a diverse photography section. The striking structure, designed by Swiss architect Mario Botta, consists of a stepped-back, sienna brick facade and a central tower constructed of alternating bands of black and white stone. Inside, natural light from the tower floods the central atrium and some of the museum's galleries. SFMOMA's café, accessible from the street, provides a comfortable, reasonably priced refuge for drinks and light meals. ⊠ *151 3rd St.,* ☎ *415/357–4000.* ☞ *$7; free 1st Tues. of each month.* ☉ *Mon.–Tues. and Fri.–Sun. 11–6, Thurs. 11–9 (½-price entry 6–9).*

★ ❿ **Yerba Buena Gardens.** This newly developed complex now ranks among San Francisco's most visually stunning areas. It's surrounded by a circular walkway lined with benches and sculptures. The waterfall memorial to Martin Luther King Jr. is the focal point of the gardens: Powerful streams of water surge over large, jagged stone columns, mirroring the enduring force of King's words that are carved on the stone walls and on glass blocks behind the waterfall. Above the memorial are two restaurants and an overhead walkway to Moscone Center's main entrance. ⊠ *Between 3rd, 4th, Mission, and Howard Sts.* ☉ *Sunrise–10 PM.*

The Financial District and Jackson Square

When San Francisco was a brawling, boozing, whoring, extravagant upstart of a town in the latter half of the 19th century, Jackson Square and the Financial District were at the heart of the action. It was on Montgomery Street that Sam Brannan proclaimed the historic gold discovery on the American River in 1848. The gold rush brought streams of people from across America and Europe, transforming the onetime frontier town into a cosmopolitan city almost overnight. Along with the prospectors came other fortune seekers: Saloon keepers, gamblers, and prostitutes flocked to the so-called Barbary Coast. Underground dance halls, casinos, bordellos, and palatial homes sprung up as the city grew to 250,000 in only a quarter of a century. Along with the quick money came a wave of violence: Diarists commented that hardly a day would pass without bloodshed, and "houses of ill-repute" proliferated. As one Frenchman noted: "There are also some honest women in San Francisco, but not very many."

By 1917 the excesses of the Barbary Coast had fallen victim to the Red-Light Abatement Act and the ire of church leaders—the young city was forced to grow up. Jackson Square is now a sedate district of refurbished brick buildings housing high-end antiques shops and architecture firms. The bay has been filled in, and the Financial District has grown into a congested canyon of soaring skyscrapers, gridlocked traffic, and bustling pedestrians. Only one remnant of the gold rush era remains: Under building foundations along the former wharf-dominated streets between California and Broadway, at least 100 ships lay abandoned by frantic crews caught up in gold fever.

There are 50 sites along the official, 3¾-mi-long Barbary Coast Trail that begins at the Old Mint, at 5th and Mission streets, and runs north to the Northern Waterfront. Its most interesting highlights start at Montgomery and Market streets.

Sights to See

⑲ **Bank of America.** This 52-story polished red granite-and-marble building dominates nearly an entire block. On the Kearny and California streets corner a massive, abstract black-granite sculpture designed by the Japanese artist Masayuki is dubbed "The Banker's Heart" by local wags. Inside are small exhibits of impressive original art. At the top of the complex is the **Carnelian Room** (☎ 415/433–7500), a chic cocktail lounge and restaurant with a great sunset and nighttime view. By day the room is open only to members of the exclusive Banker's Club. ⊠ *Between California, Pine, Montgomery, and Kearny Sts.*

㉒ **Jackson Square.** Here was the heart of the Barbary Coast of the Gay '90s. Though most of the red-light district was destroyed in the 1906 fire, the old redbrick buildings and narrow alleys recall the romance and rowdiness of the early days. Some of the city's earliest business buildings survived the 1906 quake and still stand in Jackson Square, between Montgomery and Sansome streets. Four 1850s buildings stand along the 700 block of Montgomery Street.

In 1951 a group of preservation-minded designers and furniture wholesale dealers selected the then depressed area for their showrooms, turning Jackson Square into the interior design center of the West. By the 1970s the renovated brick buildings were acclaimed nationwide. In 1972 the city officially designated the area San Francisco's first historic district. Seventeen buildings were given landmark status. When property values soared, many of the fabric and furniture outlets were forced to move to the developing Potrero Hill neighborhood. Advertising agencies, attorneys, and antiques dealers now occupy the charming renovations.

The tiny alley connecting Washington and Jackson streets is named for the head of the **A. P. Hotaling Company whiskey distillery,** which was at 451 Jackson and had the largest liquor repository on the West Coast. The alley is lined with charming, restored 19th-century brick buildings, so take your time wandering through. The old Hotaling building has unfortunately been painted a dull green and reveals little of its infamous past. A plaque on the side of the building repeats a famous query about its surviving the quake: IF, AS THEY SAY, GOD SPANKED THE TOWN FOR BEING OVER FRISKY, WHY DID HE BURN THE CHURCHES DOWN AND SAVE HOTALING'S WHISKY? ⊠ *Between Washington, Broadway, Montgomery, and Sansome Sts.*

⑱ Pacific Stock Exchange. Ralph Stackpole's monumental 1930 granite sculptural groups, *Earth's Fruitfulness* and *Man's Inventive Genius,* flank this imposing structure, which dates from 1915. The Stock Exchange Tower, around the corner at 155 Sansome Street, is a 1930 modern classic by architects Miller and Pfleuger, with an art deco gold ceiling and a black marble wall entry. ⊠ *301 Pine St. (tower around corner at 155 Sansome St.).*

㉓ San Francisco Brewing Company. Built in 1907, this pub looks like a museum piece from the Barbary Coast days.

An old upright piano sits in the corner under the original stained-glass windows. Take a seat at the beautiful mahogany bar and look down at the white-tile spittoon. In an adjacent room look for the handmade copper brewing kettle, now used to produce a dozen beers—with names like Pony Express—using old-fashioned gravity-flow methods. ⊠ *155 Columbus Ave.*, ☎ *415/434–3344.*

㉑ **Transamerica Pyramid.** The city's most photographed highrise is the 853-ft Transamerica Pyramid. Designed by William Pereira and Associates in 1972, the controversial $34 million symbol has become more acceptable to local purists over time. The 27th floor viewing area has been closed for several years. A fragrant redwood grove along the east side of the building, replete with benches and a cheerful fountain, is a nice place to unwind. Vertigo, the ground-floor restaurant (☞ Mediterranean *in* Chapter 3), has an amazing heads-up view of the tower. ⊠ *600 Montgomery St.*

㉒ **Wells Fargo Bank History Museum.** Detailing the history of the gold rush days, this museum makes a quick but interesting stop. There were no formal banks in San Francisco during the early years of the gold rush, and miners often entrusted their gold dust to saloon keepers. In 1852 Wells Fargo opened its first bank in the city, and established offices in the mother lode camps, using stagecoaches and pony express riders to service the growing state. (California's population boomed from 15,000 to 200,000 between 1848 and 1852.) The museum displays samples of nuggets and gold dust from mines, a mural-size map of the Mother Lode, original art by western artists Charlie Russell and Maynard Dixon, mementos of the poet bandit Black Bart ("Po8," as he signed his poems), and an old telegraph machine on which you can practice sending codes. The showpiece is the red Concord stagecoach that in the mid-1850s carried 18 passengers from St. Joseph, Missouri, to San Francisco in three weeks. ⊠ *420 Montgomery St.*, ☎ *415/396–2619.* 🎟 *Free.* ☉ *Weekdays 9–5.*

Chinatown

Prepare to have all your senses assaulted as you enter Chinatown: Pungent smells waft out of restaurants, fish markets, and produce stands; good-luck banners of crimson and gold hang beside dragon-entwined lampposts, pagoda roofs, and street signs with Chinese calligraphy; honking cars chime in with shoppers bargaining loudly in Cantonese or Mandarin.

Bordered roughly by Bush, Kearny, Powell, and Broadway, Chinatown is home to one of the largest Chinese communities outside Asia and to recent Southeast Asian immigrants. The two main drags of Chinatown are Grant Avenue, where most of the tourist shops reside, and Stockton Street, where the locals do their business. On Stockton, housewives jostle one another as they pick apart sidewalk displays of Chinese vegetables; double-parked trucks unloading crates of chickens add to the all-day traffic jams (don't bring a car here); and excellent examples of Chinese architecture line the street. Almost 100 restaurants offer some of the best Chinese regional cooking in the United States, whether Cantonese cuisine or the spicier Szechuan, Hunan, and Mandarin specialties.

Merely strolling through Chinatown yields endless pleasures, but you'll have a better chance of experiencing an authentic bit of one of the world's oldest cultures by venturing off the beaten track. You needn't be shy about stepping into a temple or an herb shop: Chinatown has been a tourist stop for more than 100 years, and most of its residents welcome guests.

Sights to See

㉔ Chinatown Gate. This pagoda-topped gate, flanked on either side of Grant Avenue by stone dragons, is the official entrance to Chinatown. Note that the dragons are stamped MADE IN FREE CHINA—a not-so-subdued political statement. ⊠ *Bush St. and Grant Ave.*

Chinatown YWCA. This handsome redbrick building was originally a meeting place and residence for Chinese women in need of social services. A large lantern welcomes you through its arched doorway; inside, the lobby hearkens back to early 20th-century Chinatown, with heavy, filigreed wood furniture and mirrors etched with delicate calligraphy. Julia Morgan, the architect of the famous Hearst Castle, at San Simeon, California, designed this YWCA. ⊠ *965 Clay St.*

26 Chinese Culture Center. This community organization displays the work of Chinese and Chinese-American artists as well as traveling exhibits relating to Chinese culture. Walking tours ($15) of historic points in Chinatown can be arranged on Saturday and Sunday at 2. ⊠ *Holiday Inn, 750 Kearny St., 3rd floor,* ☎ *415/986–1822.* ☒ *Free.* ☉ *Tues.–Sun. 10–4.*

27 Chinese Historical Society. This careworn but important museum documents the little-publicized history of Chinese immigrants and their descendants from the early 1800s to the present. Beginning with the treatment of the "coolies" (Chinese indentured laborers), the exhibit traces the struggles of miners and railroad workers and the activists' fights for early civil rights legislation. ⊠ *650 Commercial St.,* ☎ *415/391–1188 (move to 965 Clay St. scheduled for fall 1998).* ☒ *Free.* ☉ *Tues.–Fri. 10–4, Sat. 11–2.*

Chinese Six Companies. This is the most noteworthy example of Chinese architecture on Stockton Street. With its curved roof tiles and elaborate cornices, the imposing structure's oversize pagoda cheerfully dominates the block. The business leaders who ran the six companies dominated Chinatown's political and economic life for decades. ⊠ *843 Stockton St.*

NEED A BREAK? Dim sum, a variety of pastries filled with meat, fish, and vegetables, is the Chinese version of a brunchtime smorgasbord. In most dim sum restaurants women navigate stacked food-service carts from which customers make selections. The final bill is tabulated by the number of different saucers on the table. A favorite is **New Asia** (⊠ 772 Pacific Ave., ☎ 415/391-6666), where dim sum is available daily from 8:30 AM to 9 PM.

30 Kong Chow Temple. The temple, established in 1851, is now in a modern building; take the elevator up to the fourth floor where you will be greeted by the scent of incense. Amid the statuary, flowers, orange offerings, and richly colored altars (red signifies "virility," green "longevity," and gold "majesty") is a plaque announcing that MRS. HARRY S. TRUMAN CAME TO THIS TEMPLE IN JUNE 1948 FOR A PREDICTION ON THE OUTCOME OF THE ELECTION. . . . THIS FORTUNE CAME

TRUE. You can show your respect by placing a dollar bill in the donation box. ⊠ *855 Stockton St.*

㉘ Old Chinese Telephone Exchange. The original Chinatown burned down after the 1906 earthquake, and this was the first building to set the style for the new Chinatown. The intricate three-tier pagoda, now the Bank of Canton, was built in 1909. The exchange's operators were renowned for their tenacious memories, about which the San Francisco Chamber of Commerce boasted in 1914: "These girls respond all day with hardly a mistake to calls that are given (in English or one of five Chinese dialects) by the name of the subscriber instead of by his number—a mental feat that would be practically impossible to most high-schooled American misses." ⊠ *743 Washington St.*

㉕ Old St. Mary's Church. This building, whose structure includes granite quarried in China, was dedicated in 1854 and served as the city's Catholic cathedral until 1891. The cathedral hosts a Noontime Concert series every Tuesday and Thursday at 12:30. Across California Street is **St. Mary's Park,** a tranquil setting for local sculptor Beniamino (Benny) Bufano's *Sun Yat-sen.* The 12-ft statue of the founder of the Republic of China was installed in 1937 on the site of the Chinese leader's favorite reading spot during his years of exile in San Francisco. ⊠ *Grant Ave. and California St.,* ☎ *415/288–3840 (concert line).* ⊠ *$3 suggested donation for concert series.*

Portsmouth Square. This former potato patch that became the plaza for Yerba Buena (the Mexican settlement that was later renamed San Francisco) is also where Montgomery raised the American flag in 1846. The bronze galleon atop a 9-ft granite shaft, designed by Bruce Porter, was erected in 1919 in memory of Robert Louis Stevenson, who often visited the site during his 1879–80 residence. Dotted with pagoda-shaped structures, the park is a favorite spot for morning tai chi. By noon dozens of men huddle around Chinese chess tables, engaged in not-always-legal competition. A sand-covered playground sits below the main level of the square. ⊠ *Kearny St. between Washington and Clay Sts.*

㉙ Tien Hou Temple. Waverly Place is full of ornate painted balconies and Chinese temples, and Tien Hou is one of its best examples. Day Ju, one of the first three Chinese to arrive in San Francisco, dedicated the temple to the Queen of the Heavens and the Goddess of the Seven Seas in 1852. Climb three flights of stairs past two mah-jongg parlors whose patrons hope the spirits above will favor them. In the entryway elderly ladies can often be seen preparing "money" to be burned as offerings to various Buddhist gods. A (real) dollar placed in the donation box on their table will bring a smile (and is expected). Red-and-gold lanterns adorn the ceiling. A wood carving suspended from the ceiling depicts gods at play. ⊠ *125 Waverly Pl.* ☉ *Daily 10–4.*

North Beach and Telegraph Hill

The corner of Columbus Avenue and Broadway is a dividing line between Chinatown and North Beach, the city's most vibrant and established neighborhoods. Novelist and resident Herbert Gold calls North Beach "the longest-running, most glorious American bohemian operetta outside Greenwich Village." Indeed, to anyone who's spent time in its eccentric old bars and cafés or wandered its charming side streets and steep alleys, North Beach evokes everything from the wild Barbary Coast days to the no-less-sedate beatnik era. You can still find family operettas performed at Caffè Trieste (opened in 1956), Italian bakeries that appear frozen in time, homages to Jack Kerouac and Allen Ginsberg at every turn, and the modern equivalent of the Barbary Coast's "houses of ill-repute" in the strip joints on Broadway.

Like Chinatown, this is a neighborhood where eating is unavoidable: The streets are packed with savory Italian delicatessens, bakeries, Chinese markets, coffeehouses, and ethnic restaurants. A local delicacy is focaccia—spongy, pizzalike bread slathered with olive oil and chives or tomato sauce—sold fresh from the oven at places like quaint old Danilo Bakery (⊠ 516 Green St., near Grant Ave., ☎ 415/989–1806). Eaten warm or cold, it's the perfect walking food.

Though one associates seafood with nearby Fisherman's Wharf, fishing was North Beach's first industry. Among the first immigrants to Yerba Buena during the early 1840s were young men from the northern provinces of Italy, when this area was truly a beach (at the time of the gold rush the bay extended into the hollow between Telegraph and Russian hills). The Genoese started the still-active fishing industry in the newly renamed boomtown of San Francisco, as well as a much-needed produce business. Later, Sicilians emerged as leaders of the fishing fleets and eventually as proprietors of the seafood restaurants lining Fisherman's Wharf. Less than a square mile, North Beach is now the most densely populated district in the city—and among the most cosmopolitan.

Sights to See

★ ㉟ **Coit Tower.** Among San Francisco's most distinctive skyline sights, the 180-ft-tall Coit Tower stands as a monument to the city's volunteer firefighters. During the early days of the gold rush, Lillie Hitchcock Coit (known as Miss Lil) was said to have deserted a wedding party and chased down the street after her favorite engine, Knickerbocker Number 5, while clad in her bridesmaid finery. She was soon made an honorary member of the Knickerbocker Company, and after that always signed her name as "Lillie Coit 5" in honor of her favorite fire engine. Lillie died in 1929 at the age of 86, leaving the city $125,000 of her million-dollar-plus estate to "expend in an appropriate manner . . . to the beauty of San Francisco."

Inside the tower are 19 WPA-era murals depicting labor union workers. The U.S. government commissioned the murals as a Public Works of Art project during the Depression days of the mid-1930s. At the top of the tower you'll enjoy the panoramic view of the Bay Bridge and the Golden Gate Bridge; directly offshore is famous Alcatraz, and just behind it is Angel Island, a hikers' and campers' paradise. ⊠ *On top of Telegraph Hill.* 🎫 *$3.* 🕙 *Daily 10–6.*

Grant Avenue. Today's bohemian community has migrated up Grant Avenue above Columbus Avenue. Originally called Calle de la Fundación, Grant Avenue is the oldest street in the city. Here you'll find dusty bars (the Saloon, Grant & Green Blues Club) that evoke the Wild West, odd curio shops and unusual import stores, wonderfully atmospheric cafés, and authentic Italian delis. In June a street fair trumpets the area's Italian culture. ⊠ *Between Columbus Ave. and Filbert Sts.*

NEED A
BREAK? A Saturday afternoon must is **Caffe Trieste** (⊠ 601 Vallejo
St., at Grant Ave., ☎ 415/392–6739), where the Giotta
family presents a weekly musical (patrons are encouraged
to participate). Beginning at 1:30, the program ranges from
Italian pop and folk music to favorite family operas. This
was once the headquarters of the area's beatnik poets,
artists, and writers. If you'd rather be in Sicily, drop in for a
glass of red wine before the dinner hour at **Caffe Sport** (⊠
574 Green St., near Columbus Ave., ☎ 415/981–1251),
where a wondrous spectacle of bright artifacts from the old
country hangs from the walls.

Levi Strauss headquarters. This carefully landscaped complex appears so collegiate it is affectionately known as LSU
(Levi Strauss University). Fountains and grassy knolls com-
plement the redbrick buildings, providing a perfect envi-
ronment for picnic lunches. Delis and other take-out shops
are nearby. ⊠ *Levi's Plaza, 1155 Battery St.*

㉜ St. Francis of Assisi Church. An 1860 Victorian Gothic
building with a terra-cotta facade stands on the site of the
frame parish church that served the gold-rush Catholic
community. ⊠ *610 Vallejo St.*

㉝ Saints Peter and Paul. The Disney-esque twin turrets of this
Romanesque cathedral are local landmarks. On the first Sunday of October a mass and a parade to Fisherman's Wharf
are part of the annual Blessing of the Fleet. Another popular annual event is the Columbus Day pageant. ⊠ *666 Filbert St., at Washington Square Park.*

㉞ Telegraph Hill. Telegraph Hill residents command some of
the best views in the city, as well as the most difficult as-
cents to their aeries (the charming flower-lined steps flank-
ing the hill make the climb more than tolerable for visitors,
though). The hill rises from the east end of Lombard Street
to about 300 ft and is capped with the landmark Coit
Tower (☞ *above*). ⊠ *Between Lombard, Filbert, Kearny,
and Sansome Sts.*

㉛ Washington Square. This may well be the daytime social
heart of what was once considered Little Italy—though in
the early morning the dominating sight is of a hundred or
more elderly Asians engaged in tai chi. By mid-morning

groups of elderly Italian men arrive to sun and sigh at the state of their immediate world. Nearby, kids toss Frisbees, jugglers juggle, and elderly Chinese matrons stare impassively at the passing parade. ⊠ *Between Columbus Ave., Stockton, Filbert, and Union Sts.*

Nob Hill and Russian Hill

Once called the Hill of Golden Promise, this area was officially dubbed Nob Hill during the 1870s when "the Big Four"—Charles Crocker, Leland Stanford, Mark Hopkins, and Collis Huntington—built their hilltop estates. Nob Hill is still home to many of the city's elite, as well as many of San Francisco's finest hotels. Though it lacks the quirky flavor of many other San Francisco neighborhoods, it exudes a sense of history. If you don't mind climbing uphill, Nob Hill is within walking distance of Union Square. Otherwise, the cable car runs up California Street.

Just nine blocks or so from downtown (and a few blocks north of Nob Hill), Russian Hill has long been home to old San Francisco families, and during the 1890s, to a group of bohemian artists and writers that included Charles Norris, George Sterling, and Maynard Dixon. The hills are covered with an astounding array of housing: simple studios, sumptuous pieds-à-terre, Victorian flats, quaint Edwardian cottages, and costly boxlike condos. The bay views here are some of the best, and the neighborhood is home to the renowned San Francisco Art Institute and several excellent restaurants (especially on Hyde Street).

Sights to See

39 Cable Car Museum. This is a brief but engaging stopover on the way to Russian Hill. On exhibit are photographs, old cable cars, signposts, ticketing machines, and other memorabilia dating from 1873. The four sets of massive powerhouse wheels that move the entire cable car system steal the show: The design is so simple it seems almost unreal. You can also go downstairs and check out the innards of the system. A 15-minute video describes how it works (cables must be replaced every 75 to 250 days!). ⊠ *1201 Mason St., at Washington St.,* ☎ *415/474–1887.* ☜ *Free.* ⊙ *Oct.–Mar., daily 10–5; Apr.–Sept., daily 10–6.*

Fairmont Hotel. The Fairmont's dazzling opening was delayed a year by the 1906 quake, but since then the marble palace has hosted presidents, royalty, movie stars (Valentino, Dietrich), and local nabobs. Nowadays, prices run as high as $6,000 for a night in an eight-room, Persian art–filled penthouse suite. Treat yourself to afternoon tea in the lobby Monday–Saturday 3–6 and Sunday 1–6: Designed by Dorothy Draper in 1947, it has flamboyant rose-floral carpeting, lush red-velvet chairs, gold faux-marble columns, and gilt ceilings. The hotel's kitschy **Tonga Room,** (☞ San Francisco's Favorite Bars *in* Chapter 5) is a hoot. ✉ *950 Mason St.,* ☎ *415/772–5000.*

④¹ Feusier House. Built in 1857, this octagonal private residence is surrounded by lush gardens and can only be viewed from the street. Across from the Feusier House is the **1907 Firehouse** (✉ 1088 Green St.). Local art patron Mrs. Ralph K. Davies bought it from the city in 1956. It's closed to the public, so view from afar. ✉ *1067 Green St.*

③⁷ Grace Cathedral. The seat of the Episcopal Church in San Francisco, this soaring Gothic structure erected on the site of Charles Crocker's mansion took 53 years to build. The gilded bronze doors at the east entrance were taken from casts of Ghiberti's Gates of Paradise, which are on the baptistery in Florence, Italy. A gorgeous black-and-bronze stone sculpture of St. Francis by Beniamino Bufano greets visitors as they enter.

Perhaps the most unique feature of Grace is its 35-ft-wide Labyrinth, a large, purplish rug that's a replica of the 13th-century stone labyrinth on the floor of the Chartres Cathedral. All are encouraged to walk the ⅓-mi-long labyrinth, a ritual based on the tradition of meditative walking. The AIDS Memorial Chapel has a sculpture by the late artist Keith Haring and rotating panels from the AIDS Memorial Quilt. ✉ *1051 Taylor St.,* ☎ *415/749–6300.* ⊙ *Daily 7–6; gift shop Mon.–Sat. 10–5, Sun. 9:30–11 and 12:30–3:30.*

④⁰ Ina Coolbrith Park. This attractive park is composed of a series of terraces on the side of a hill. An Oakland librarian and poet, Ina Coolbrith introduced both Jack London and Isadora Duncan to the world of books. In 1915 she was named poet laureate of California. The climb to the

park is steep, so make use of the benches at various levels.
⊠ *Vallejo St. between Mason and Taylor Sts.*

★ ㊸ **Lombard Street.** San Francisco's "crookedest" street drops
down the east face of Russian Hill in eight switchbacks. Join
the line of cars waiting to drive down the steep hill, or walk
down the steps for a fine view of North Beach and Coit Tower.
⊠ *Lombard St. between Hyde and Leavenworth Sts.*

㊷ **Macondray Lane.** Enter this "secret garden" under a lovely
wooden trellis and walk down a quiet cobbled pedestrian
street lined with Edwardian cottages and flowering plants
and trees. At the end of the lane a flight of steep wooden
stairs leads down to Taylor Street—offering spectacular views
of the bay. ⊠ *Jones St. between Union and Green Sts.*

㊳ **Mark Hopkins Inter-Continental Hotel.** A combination of
French château and Spanish Renaissance architecture (with
terra-cotta detailing), this hotel has hosted statesmen, royalty, and Hollywood celebrities. From the 1920s through
the 1940s, Benny Goodman, Tommy Dorsey, and other top
entertainers appeared here regularly. The **Top of the Mark**
cocktail lounge is remembered fondly by thousands of
World War II veterans who jammed the lounge before leaving for overseas duty; wives and sweethearts watching the
ships depart gave the room's northwest nook its name—
Weepers' Corner. ⊠ *1 Nob Hill, at California and Mason
Sts.,* ☎ *415/392–3434.*

㊱ **Masonic Auditorium.** Formally called the California Masonic
Memorial Temple, this building was erected by Freemasons
in 1957. A selection of brochures by the entrance explains
the beliefs of Freemasonry. The impressive lobby mosaic
depicts the Masonic fraternity's role in California history
and industry. There's also an intricate model of King
Solomon's Temple in the lobby. ⊠ *1111 California St.,* ☎
415/776–4917. ☺ *Lobby weekdays 8–5.*

Pacific Union Club. The quake and fire of 1906 knocked
down all of Nob Hill's palatial mansions save one: the
shell of the Flood brownstone. This attractive broad-beam,
structure was built by the Comstock silver baron at a re-
puted cost of $1.5 million. In 1909 the property was pur-
chased by the Pacific Union Club, a bastion of the wealthy

and powerful. Adjacent is a charming small park noted for its frequent art shows. ✉ *1000 California St.*

Pre-quake buildings. A number of buildings in this neighborhood survived the 1906 earthquake and fire and still stand today: The house at **1652–1656 Taylor Street,** and several brown-shingle structures on Vallejo Street designed by Willis Polk, one of the city's most famous architects. Look for **1013 Vallejo Street,** where the Polk family resided for years, and **1034–1036 Vallejo,** just beyond. ✉ *On and adjacent to Vallejo steps between Taylor and Jones Sts.*

Russian Hill alleys. **Russian Hill Place** has a row of quaint Mediterranean-style town houses designed by Willis Polk in 1915. On **Florence Place** several 1920s stucco survivors reign over more contemporary construction. ✉ *Vallejo St. near Jones St.*

44 San Francisco Art Institute. A Moorish-tiled fountain in a pleasant tree-shaded courtyard greets you as you enter the institute, which bustles with students during the week. The institute dates to 1871, and Spanish colonial-style building was erected on Russian Hill in 1926.

The institute has long been known for its innovation, with the country's first fine arts film program, and with Ansel Adams creating the school's fine arts photography department in 1946. Notable faculty and alumni have included Dorothea Lange, Edward Weston, Richard Diebenkorn, James Weeks, and Annie Leibovitz. Works by students line the walls, and the McBean Gallery exhibits provocative work by more established artists. Don't miss the impressive seven-section fresco painted in 1931 by Mexican master Diego Rivera, it's in the student gallery to the left as you enter the institute; it's one of three Bay Area murals painted by Rivera. The Art Institute Café has a view of Alcatraz and the bay. ✉ *800 Chestnut St.,* ☏ *415/771–7020.* ▱ *Gallery free.* ☉ *McBean Gallery Tues.–Sat. 10–5 (Thurs. until 8), Sun. noon–5; student gallery daily 9–9.*

Pacific Heights

Some of the city's most expensive and dramatic real estate—including mansions and town houses priced at $1 million and up—is in Pacific Heights. Old money and new, personalities in the limelight, and those who prefer absolute media anonymity live here. Grand old face-lifted Victorians, facades of Queen Anne charmers, English Tudor imports, and baroque bastions line the streets, and from almost any point in this neighborhood you get a magnificent view.

Sights to See

Alta Plaza Park. Landscape architect John McLaren (who also created Golden Gate Park) designed Alta Plaza in 1910, modeling its terracing on the Grand Casino in Monte Carlo, Monaco. From the top you can see Marin to the north, downtown to the east, Twin Peaks to the south, and Golden Gate Park to the west. ✉ *Between Clay, Steiner, Jackson, and Scott Sts.*

㊼ **Broadway estates.** Broadway uptown (unlike its North Beach stretch) is home to some prestigious addresses, including a consulate and several classic showplaces. At **2222 Broadway** is a three-story palace with an intricately filigreed doorway built by Comstock mine heir James Flood and later donated to a religious order. The Convent of the Sacred Heart purchased the Grant House at **2220 Broadway.** These two buildings, along with a Flood property at **2120 Broadway** are all used as school quarters. ✉ *Broadway between Fillmore and Buchanan Sts.*

(51) **Franklin Street buildings.** Don't be fooled by the **Golden Gate Church** (✉ 1901 Franklin St.)—what at first looks like a stone facade is actually redwood painted white. At **1735 Franklin** you'll find a Georgian built in the early 1900s for a coffee merchant. On the northeast corner of Franklin and California streets is a **Christian Science church**; built in the Tuscan Revival style, it's noteworthy for its terracotta detailing. The **Coleman House** (✉ 1701 Franklin St.), now housing law offices, is an impressive twin-turreted mansion built for a gold rush mining and lumber baron. Don't miss the beautiful, large stained-glass window on the north side of the Coleman House. ✉ *Franklin St. between Washington and California Sts.*

㊿ **Haas-Lilienthal House.** This 1886 Queen Anne survived the 1906 earthquake and fire and is the only fully furnished Victorian open to the public. The carefully kept rooms provide an intriguing glimpse of turn-of-the-century taste and lifestyle. A small display of photographs on the bottom floor proves this elaborate house was modest compared with some of the giants that fell to the fire. ⊠ *2007 Franklin St., near Washington St.,* ☎ *415/441–3004.* 💳 *$5.* ⊙ *Wed. noon–4 (last tour at 3), Sun. 11–5 (last tour at 4). Pacific Heights tours ($5) leave the house Sun. at 12:30.*

Lafayette Park. Clusters of trees dot this four-block-square oasis for sunbathers and dog-and-Frisbee teams. During the 1860s a tenacious squatter, Sam Holladay, built himself a big wooden house in the center of the park. Holladay even instructed city gardeners as if the land were his own and defied all orders to leave. The house was finally torn down in 1936. ⊠ *Between Laguna, Gough, Sacramento, and Washington Sts.*

❺❷ Noteworthy Victorians. Two stunning **Italianate Victorians** (⊠ 1818 and 1834 California St.) stand out on the 1800 block of California. A block farther is the Victorian-era **Atherton House** (⊠ 1990 California St.), featuring one of Pacific Heights' more unusual combinations of architectural elements, including Queen Anne and Stick-Eastlake. The **Laguna Street Victorians,** on the west side of the 1800 block of Laguna Street, cost only $2,000–$2,600 when they were built in the 1870s. ⊠ *California St. between Franklin and Octavia Sts.;* ⊠ *Laguna St. between Pine and Bush Sts.*

❹❺ Octagon House. Once thought to bring good luck, eight-sided homes were popular in the mid-19th century. This one sits across the street from its original site on Gough Street. It's full of antique American furniture and decorative arts (paintings, silver, rugs) from the 18th and 19th centuries. A favorite is a deck of revolutionary-era hand-painted playing cards: In place of kings, queens, and jacks, the American upstarts substituted American statesmen, Roman goddesses, and Indian chiefs. White quoins accent each of the eight corners of the pretty blue-gray exterior. An award-winning colonial-style garden completes the picture. ⊠ *2645 Gough St., at Union St.,* ☎ *415/441–7512.* 💳 *Free; donations encouraged.* ⊙ *Feb.–Dec., 2nd Sun. and 2nd and 4th Thurs. of each month, noon–3; group tours weekdays by appointment.*

49 Spreckels Mansion. This estate was built for sugar heir Adolph Spreckels and his wife, Alma. Mrs. Spreckels was so pleased with her house that she commissioned architect George Applegarth to design another building just like it: the city's European museum, the California Palace of the Legion of Honor, in Lincoln Park. One of the city's great iconoclasts, Alma Spreckels herself is the model for the bronze figure atop the Victory Monument in Union Square. ⊠ *2080 Washington St., at Octavia St.*

46 Vedanta Society. This 1905 architectural cocktail, the first Hindu temple in the West, may be the most unusual structure in a city of unusual structures: It's a pastiche of colonial, Queen Anne, Moorish, and Hindu opulence, with turrets battling onion domes and Victorian detailing. The highest of the six Hindu systems of religious philosophy, Vedanta maintains that all religions are paths to one goal. Although its main location is at Vallejo and Fillmore streets, the Webster Street temple is Vedanta's heart. You can attend a free Friday evening class here on Hindu scriptures at 8, which begins with a half hour of meditation. ⊠ *2963 Webster St., at Filbert St.,* ☎ *415/922–2323 for viewings by request.*

Wedding Houses. These identical, white double-peaked homes (joined in the middle) were erected in the late 1870s or early 1880s by dairy rancher James Cudworth as wedding gifts for his two daughters. These days, the Siamese buildings house businesses and an English-style pub below. ⊠ *1980 Union St., at Buchanan St.,* ☎ *415/921–0300.*

48 Whittier Mansion. This was one of the most elegant 19th-century houses in the state, with a Spanish-tiled roof and enormous scrolled bay windows on all four sides. An anomaly in a town that lost most of its grand mansions to the 1906 quake, the Whittier Mansion was built so solidly that only a chimney toppled over during the disaster. ⊠ *2090 Jackson St., at Laguna St.*

Civic Center

City Hall and the cluster of handsome adjoining cultural institutions that make up San Francisco's Civic Center stand as one of the country's great governmental building complexes—a seeming realization of the visions put forth by turn-of-the-century proponents of the "city beautiful." But illusion soon gives way to reality: On the streets and plazas of the Civic Center, you'll find many of the city's most destitute residents, and much of the area is undergoing seismic retrofitting in the wake of the 1989 Loma Prieta earthquake.

East of city hall is United Nations Plaza, a bustling carnival of bright colors during the twice-weekly farmers' market. The handsome new main library is just a block west of the plaza. On the west side of city hall are the opera house, the symphony hall, and several other cultural institutions. A few upscale restaurants in the surrounding blocks cater to the theater/symphony crowd. And a couple blocks southwest on Hayes Street between Franklin and Laguna streets, a bohemian enclave of fine contemporary and ethnic art galleries, boutiques, and restaurants has been burgeoning ever since the dismantling of the overhead freeway ramp after the '89 earthquake—but be careful not to stray past Gough Street after nightfall.

Sights to See

⑤⑤ **City Hall.** This French Renaissance Revival masterpiece of granite and marble was modeled after the Capitol in Washington, D.C. (and its dome is even higher). In front are formal gardens with fountains, walkways, and seasonal flower beds. The palatial interior is scheduled to reopen after an extensive seismic upgrade in late 1998. ⊠ *Between Van Ness Ave., Polk, Grove, and McAllister Sts.*

⑤⑧ **Louise M. Davies Symphony Hall.** The 2,750-seat hall designed with sleek, futuristic wonders is the home of the San Francisco Symphony, which is led by Michael Tilson Thomas. It took several years to sort out the modern structure's acoustical problems, the solutions to which are discussed on docent-led tours. The adjacent Performing Arts Center consists of the ballet building and the Herbst Theatre. ⊠ *201 Van Ness Ave.,* ☎ *415/552–8338.* ☞ *Tours $3.* ☉ *Tours of Davies Hall Wed. and Sat. by appointment, tours of Davies and the Performing Arts Center Mon. hourly 10–2.*

San Francisco Performing Arts Library and Museum. Known as PALM, this small center mostly functions as a library and research center; it houses the largest collection of its kind on the West Coast, with more than 8,000 books and periodicals and about 2,000 radio interviews with performers. A gallery holds a quarterly exhibition of the museum's collection of programs, photographs, manuscripts, costumes, and other memorabilia of historic performance events. ⊠ *399 Grove St., at Gough St.,* ☎ *415/255–4800.* ▨ *Free.* ☉ *Wed.–Sat.; call for hrs.*

54 **San Francisco Public Library.** The new main library, which opened in April 1996, is a striking, modernized version of the old beaux arts library that sits just across Fulton Street (that building will become the new site of the Asian Art Museum). Additions include an auditorium for presentations and performances, an art gallery, a café, centers for the hearing and visually impaired, a gay and lesbian history center, African-American and Asian centers, and a rooftop garden and terrace. The new San Francisco History Room and Archives contains a wealth of historic photographs, maps, and other memorabilia. At the library's center is a five-story atrium with a skylight, a grand staircase, and murals painted by local artists. ⊠ *Larkin St. between Grove and Fulton Sts.,* ☎ *415/557–4440 or 415/557–4567 for archives hrs.* ☉ *Mon. 10–6, Tues.–Thurs. 9–8, Fri. 11–5, Sat. 9–5, Sun. noon–5.*

53 **United Nations Plaza.** The redbrick plaza is lined with brick pillars listing various nations and the dates of their admittance into the United Nations, and the floor is inscribed with the goals and philosophy of the United Nations charter. On Wednesday and Sunday a farmers' market fills the space with homegrown produce and plants. ⊠ *Fulton St. between Hyde and Market Sts.*

56 **Veterans Building.** Once home to the San Francisco Museum of Modern Art, this grand old structure that hosted the signing of the United Nations charter in 1945 still holds **Herbst Theatre** (☎ 415/392–4400)—a popular venue for lectures and performances. Of particular interest are the City Arts and Lectures events. Tickets are often available on the day of the event, though tickets to hear famous guests can sell out months in advance. The **San Francisco Arts Commission Gallery** (☎ 415/554–6080), on the bottom floor at street level, displays the works of Bay Area artists from the traditional to the avant-garde. ⊠ *401 Van Ness Ave.*

57 **War Memorial Opera House.** During San Francisco's Barbary Coast days, opera goers smoked cigars, didn't check their revolvers, and expressed their appreciation with "shrill whistles and savage yells." All the old opera houses were destroyed in the quake, but lusty support for opera continued, with coloratura soprano Luisa Tetrazzini singing in front of Lotta's Fountain on Market Street on Christmas Eve 1910 to a reported crowd of 300,000.

This 1932 opera house is modeled after its European counterparts, with a vaulted and coffered ceiling, marble foyer, two balconies, and an unusual art deco chandelier that resembles a huge silver sunburst. The San Francisco Opera and Ballet companies perform here. ✉ *301 Van Ness Ave.,* ☎ *415/621–6600.*

The Northern Waterfront

For the sights, sounds, and smells of the sea, hop the Powell-Hyde cable car from Union Square and take it to the end of the line. The views as you descend Hyde Street down to the bay are nothing short of breathtaking—tiny sailboats bob in the whitecaps, Alcatraz hovers ominously in the distance, and the Marin Headlands form a rugged backdrop to the fog-shrouded Golden Gate Bridge. Once you reach sea level at the cable car turnaround, Aquatic Park and the National Maritime Museum are immediately to the west; Fort Mason, with its several interesting museums, is just a bit farther west. For more commercial attractions, head to nearby redbrick Ghirardelli Square or to Fisherman's Wharf. Be sure to bring good walking shoes and a jacket or sweater for mid-afternoon breezes or foggy mists.

This area is famous for the arts and crafts that flourish on its streets. Each day an eclectic mix of more than 200 of the city's jewelers, painters, potters, photographers, and leather workers offer their wares for sale. (The majority are centered around Hyde Street Pier and Fisherman's Wharf, though you'll also find them at Union Square, Embarcadero Plaza, and the Cliff House.) Some items are from foreign factories and may be overpriced; bargaining is often a wise idea.

*Numbers in the margin correspond to numbers on the North-
ern Waterfront/Marina and the Presidio map.*

Sights to See

★ **Alcatraz Island.** The boat ride to the island is brief (15 minutes) but affords beautiful views of the city, Marin County,
and the East Bay. The audio tour, highly recommended,
includes observations of guards and prisoners about life
in one of America's most notorious penal colonies. A sep-
arate, ranger-led tour surveys the island's ecology. Plan your
schedule to include at least three hours for the visit and
boat rides combined. Advance reservations, even in the off-
season, are strongly recommended. ⊠ *Pier 41,* ☎ *415/546–
2628 or 415/546–2700 for tickets.* 🎫 *$11 or $7.75
without audio; add $2 per ticket to charge by phone at
415/546–2700.* 🕙 *Ferry departures Sept. 1–May 23, daily
9:30–2:15; May 24–Aug. 31, daily 9:30–4:15.*

❹ Cannery. This three-story structure was built in 1894 to
house what became the Del Monte Fruit and Vegetable Cannery. Today the Cannery is home to shops, art galleries, a
premier comedy club (Cobb's), unusual restaurants, and the
Museum of the City of San Francisco (☎ 415/928–0289),
on the third floor. ⊠ *2801 Leavenworth St.,* ☎ *415/771–
3112.* 🕙 *Mon.–Sat. 10–6, Sun. 11–6; until 8:30 Thurs.–Sat.
in summer (restaurants open later).*

NEED A
BREAK?

The mellow **Buena Vista Café** (⊠ 2765 Hyde St., ☎
415/474–5044) claims to be the first U.S. establishment to
serve Irish coffee. The café opens at 9 AM weekdays, 8 AM
weekends, and serves a great breakfast. It is always
crowded, but try for a table overlooking nostalgic Victorian
Park with its cable car turntable.

Ferries. Cruises are an exhilarating way to see the bay.
Among those offered by the **Red and White Fleet** (Pier
43½, ☎ 415/546–2628) are frequent one-hour swings
under the Golden Gate Bridge and along the Northern Waterfront. More interesting—and just as scenic—are the
tours to Sausalito, Angel Island, Alcatraz, Tiburon, Muir
Woods, and the Napa Valley Wine Country. The **Blue and
Gold Fleet** (⊠ Pier 39, ☎ 415/705–5555) conducts daily
1¼-hour tours under both the Bay and Golden Gate bridges,

as well as Friday- and Saturday-night dinner-dance cruises (reservations required) from late April until mid-December. Blue and Gold also runs ferries to Oakland, Alameda, and Vallejo. ⊠ *Fisherman's Wharf, between Piers 43½ and 39.*

❻ Fisherman's Wharf. By mid-afternoon the fishing fleet is back to port. The chaotic streets of the wharf are home to numerous seafood restaurants—including sidewalk crab pots and counters where take-out shrimp and crab cocktails are sold—and dozens of tourist magnets. T-shirts and sweats, gold chains galore, redwood furniture, and acres of artwork (some original) beckon visitors. So-called novelty museums, among them **Ripley's Believe It or Not** (⊠ 175 Jefferson St., ☎ 415/771–6188) and the **Wax Museum** (⊠ 145 Jefferson St., ☎ 415/885–4975)—along with amusing street artists—provide diversions for all ages. The World War II submarine USS *Pampanito* (☎ 415/441–5819), at Pier 45, provides a fascinating (if claustrophobic) look at life down under during wartime. The detailed audio tour is worthwhile. ⊠ *Jefferson St. between Leavenworth St. and Pier 39.*

❶ Fort Mason. Originally a depot for the shipment of supplies to the Pacific during World War II, Fort Mason was converted into a cultural center in 1977 and now houses the popular vegetarian restaurant Greens (☞ Vegetarian *in* Chapter 3) and a cornucopia of shops, galleries, and performance spaces, most of which are closed on Monday. Don't be put off by the imposing look of the warehouses; the sights within are worthwhile.

The **Mexican Museum** (⊠ Bldg. D, ☎ 415/441–0404) was the first American showcase to be devoted exclusively to Mexican, Mexican-American, and Chicano art, with everything from pre-Columbian Indian terra-cotta figures to rotating exhibits on issues of Mexican-American and Chicano culture. All explanatory text is in Spanish and English. Limited exhibition space accommodates only a fraction of the permanent collection, including a recently acquired 500-piece folk-art collection, a gift from the Nelson A. Rockefeller estate—but plans are underway move the museum to the downtown Yerba Buena complex by 1999. La Tienda, the museum shop, stocks colorful Mexican folk art, posters, books, and catalogs from museum exhibitions.

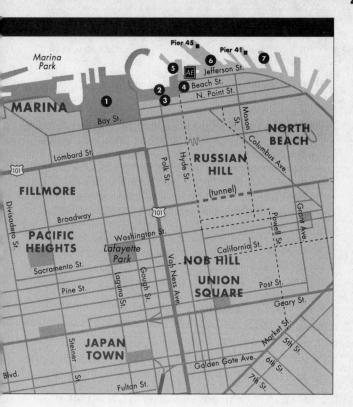

Marina
Park

MARINA

Bay St.

Lombard St.

101

FILLMORE

Broadway

101

PACIFIC
HEIGHTS

Lafayette
Park

Washington St.

Sacramento St.

Pine St.

Divisadero St.

Laguna St.

Gough St.

JAPAN
TOWN

Steiner St.

Blvd.

Fulton St.

Polk St.

Van Ness Ave.

Hyde St.

Pier 45

Pier 41

Jefferson St.

Beach St.

N. Point St.

RUSSIAN
HILL

(tunnel)

NOB HILL

UNION
SQUARE

California St.

Post St.

Geary St.

Golden Gate Ave.

Market St.

Powell St.

Grant Ave.

Mason St.

Columbus Ave.

NORTH
BEACH

5th St.

6th St.

7th St.

Also in Building D is the **Magic Theatre** (☎ 415/441–8822), a well-respected company known for producing the works of contemporary playwrights such as Sam Shepard, as well as local and national writers.

Building C houses the **Museo Italo-Americano** (☎ 415/673–2200), which hosts permanent exhibits of 19th- and 20th-century Italian-American artists, as well as rotating shows that include paintings, sculpture, etchings, and photographs. The **San Francisco African-American Historical and Cultural Society** (☎ 415/441–0640), the only museum of black culture west of the Rockies, has permanent exhibits on the history of blacks in California and in the Civil War; temporary exhibits showcase contemporary black artists from California. In Building A is the **San Francisco Craft and Folk Art Museum** (☎ 415/775–0990), a tiny space with rotating exhibits on culture and folk art from around the world and a gift shop with American folk art, tribal art, and contemporary crafts. Most of the museums and shops at Fort Mason close by 7, though the theaters and Greens restaurant stay open later. ⊠ *Buchanan St. and Marina Blvd.,* ☎ *415/979–3010 for event information.*

❸ Ghirardelli Square. This charming complex of 19th-century redbrick factory buildings—once the home of the Ghirardelli Chocolate Company— has been transformed into a network of specialty shops and eateries. Two unusual shops in the Cocoa Building are the **Xanadu Gallery** (☎ 415/441–5211) and **Folk Art International** (☎ 415/928–3340): Both display museum-quality tribal art from Asia, Africa, Oceania, and the Americas. Don't miss the **Creative Spirit Gallery** (☎ 415/441–1537), a space for disabled artists sponsored by the National Institute of Art and Disabilities; the handicrafts for sale have an unusual beauty, and 60% of the proceeds go directly to the artists. It's on the Lower Plaza level of the Cocoa Building. ⊠ *900 North Point,* ☎ *415/775–5500.* ☉ *Jan.–Mar., Sun.–Thurs. 10–6, Fri.–Sat. 10–9; April–Dec., daily 10–9.*

❺ Hyde Street Pier. The pier, one of the wharf area's best bargains, always bustles with activity. The highlight of the pier is its collection of historic vessels, all of which can be boarded: the *Balclutha,* an 1886 full-rigged, three-mast sailing vessel that sailed around Cape Horn 17 times; the

Eureka, a side-wheel ferry; the *C. A. Thayer,* a three-masted schooner; and the *Hercules,* a tugboat. ⊠ *Hyde St.,* ☎ *415/929–0202.* ☞ *$3.* ☉ *Fall–spring, daily 9:30–5; summer, daily 10–6.*

❷ National Maritime Museum. You'll feel as if you're out to sea when you step inside this sturdy, rounded structure. Part of the San Francisco Maritime National Historical Park, which includes Hyde Street Pier, the museum exhibits ship models, photographs, maps, and other artifacts chronicling the development of San Francisco and the West Coast through maritime history. ⊠ *Aquatic Park at the foot of Polk St.,* ☎ *415/556–3002 or 415/929–0202.* ☞ *Donation suggested.* ☉ *Daily 10–5.*

❼ Pier 39. This is the most popular—and the most commercial—of San Francisco's waterfront attractions, drawing millions of visitors each year to browse through its dozens of shops. Ongoing free entertainment, accessible validated parking, and nearby public transportation ensure crowds most days. Check out **Left Hand World** (☎ 415/433–3547), where you'll find all manner of gadgets designed with lefties in mind; the **Marine Mammal Store & Interpretive Center** (☎ 415/289–7373), a quality gift shop and education center whose proceeds benefit Sausalito's Marine Mammal Center; and the **National Park Store** (☎ 415/433–7221), a naturist's Eden, with numerous books, maps, and collectibles. Children shouldn't miss the brilliantly colored double-decker **Venetian Carousel.** At **Underwater World** (☎ 415/623–5300), moving walkways transport you through a space surrounded on three sides by water filled with indigenous San Francisco Bay marine life, from fish and plankton to sharks. Hundreds of sea lions bask and play on the docks on the pier's northwest side. Start your visit at the newly opened **Welcome Center,** inside the Citybank Cinemax Theater, open 9–5:30 daily. ⊠ *Pier 39 off Jefferson St.*

The Marina and the Presidio

The Marina district was a coveted place to live until the 1989 earthquake, when the area's homes suffered the worst damage in the city because the Marina is built on landfill. Although many homeowners and renters left in search of more solid ground, the Marina is still popular with young professionals. On weekends, Chestnut and Union streets are filled with a fairly homogeneous, well-to-do crowd, and the Marina Safeway is known far and wide as a pickup joint for young singles.

West of the Marina is the sprawling Presidio, a former military base that has been turned over to the Golden Gate National Recreation Area. The Presidio has stunning views and the best hiking and biking areas in San Francisco; a drive through the area can also be rewarding.

Numbers in the margin correspond to numbers on the Northern Waterfront/Marina and the Presidio map.

Sights to See

🔟 Commandante's Quarters. This low adobe structure was built during the Spanish and Mexican regimes in California and restored to its original form in 1934. When California came under U.S. control, the army continued to use it as a headquarters. Look for the plaque and old cannons in front near the awning. ⊠ *Moraga Ave. between Funston and Arguello Aves.*

🄲 Exploratorium. Within the Palace of Fine Arts, this fascinating "museum of science, art, and human perception" is as entertaining as it is educational—for both kids and adults. The curious of all ages flock here to play with and learn from some of the 600 exhibits. Be sure to crawl through the dark, touchy-feely Tactile Dome and inquire about the film and lecture program. Regular science demonstrations (lasers, dissection of a cow's eye) begin around 10:30 each day. ⊠ *Baker and Beach Sts.,* ☎ *415/561–0360 for general information or 415/561–0362 for required reservations for Tactile Dome.* ⌨ *$9; free 1st Wed. of month.* ⊙ *Tues.–Sun. 10–5, Wed. until 9:30; official Mon. holidays 10–5.*

⑫ Fort Point. Designed to mount 125 cannons, with a range of up to 2 mi, Fort Point was constructed between 1853 and 1861 to protect San Francisco from sea attack during the Civil War—but it was never used for that purpose. It was, however, used as a coastal defense fortification post during World War II. This National Historic Landmark is now a museum filled with military memorabilia. Guided group tours and cannon drills are offered daily, and the top floor has a superb view of the bay. Take care when walking along the front side of the building as it's slippery, and the waves have a dizzying effect. ⊠ *Lincoln Blvd. near Golden Gate Bridge*, ☎ *415/556–1693.* 🖾 *Free.* ☉ *Wed.–Sun. 10–5.*

★ ⑬ **Golden Gate Bridge.** Connecting San Francisco with Marin County, the Golden Gate Bridge has long wowed sightseers with its unique rust-color beauty and simple but powerful art deco design. At nearly 2 mi, it is one of the longest bridges in the world—and also one of the strongest, made to withstand winds of more than 100 mph. Though frequently gusty and misty (walkers should wear warm clothing), the bridge offers unparalleled views of the Bay Area, as does a vista point on the Marin side. ⊠ *Lincoln Blvd. near Doyle Dr. and Fort Point.*

★ ⑧ **Palace of Fine Arts.** San Francisco's rosy rococo Palace of Fine Arts is at the very edge of the Marina. The palace is the sole survivor of the many tinted plaster buildings (a temporary classical city of sorts) built for the 1915 Panama-Pacific International Exposition; the expo lasted for 288 days, and the buildings extended about a mile along the shore. Bernard Maybeck designed the Roman classic beauty, which was reconstructed in concrete and reopened in 1967, thanks to legions of sentimental citizens and a huge private donation. The massive columns, great rotunda (dedicated to the glory of Greek culture), and swan-filled lagoon have been used in countless fashion layouts and recent films. ⊠ *Baker and Beach Sts.,* ☎ *415/563–7337 for palace tours.*

⑨ **Presidio.** Currently part of the Golden Gate National Recreation Area, the Presidio was a military post for more than 200 years. Don Juan Bautista de Anza and a band of Spanish settlers first claimed the area in 1776. It became a Mexican garrison in 1822 when Mexico gained its independence from Spain, until U.S. troops forcibly occupied it in 1846. The U.S. Sixth Army was stationed here until October 1994, when the coveted space was finally transferred into civilian hands. The more than 1,400 acres of rolling hills, majestic woods, and attractive redbrick army barracks present an air of serenity in the middle of the city. There are two beaches, a golf course, and picnic sites, and the views of the bay, Golden Gate Bridge, and Marin County are sublime. The **Presidio Visitors Information Center** (⊠ Lincoln Blvd. and Montgomery St., ☎ 415/561–4323) offers maps, brochures, and schedules for guided walking and bicycle tours. It's open daily from 10 to 5. ⊠ *Between the Marina and Lincoln Park.*

⑪ Presidio Museum. This museum in a former military hospital built in 1863 focuses on the military's role in San Francisco's development. Behind it are two cabins that housed refugees from the 1906 earthquake and fire. Photos on the wall of one cabin depict rows and rows of temporary shelters at the Presidio and in Golden Gate Park following the disaster. ⊠ *Lincoln Blvd. and Funston Ave.,* ☎ *415/561–4331.* ☞ *Free.* ☉ *Wed.–Sun. 10–4.*

Golden Gate Park

In 1887 Scotsman John McLaren transformed this desolate brush- and sand-covered expanse in the central-western part of San Francisco into a rolling, beautifully landscaped 1,000-acre oasis that stretches more than 2 mi out to the ocean. Though urban and suburban life touch it on all sides, the park is a great getaway spot within the city, with everything from a playground and gardens to a tea house, a lake, and several first-rate museums.

Here you can attend a polo game or a Sunday band concert; rent a bike, boat, or Rollerblades (☞ Chapter 6); or watch players at the century-old lawn-bowling court with its 1915-era Edwardian clubhouse. On Sunday John F. Kennedy Drive is closed to cars and comes alive with joggers, bicyclists, skaters, museum goers, and picnickers. In addition, there are tennis courts, baseball diamonds, soccer fields, a buffalo paddock, and miles of trails for horseback riding.

If you plan to visit more than one attraction in the park, consider purchasing a Golden Gate Explorer Pass ($12), which grants admission to the de Young and Asian Art museums, plus the California Academy of Sciences, the Japanese Tea Garden, and (when it reopens) the Conservatory. The pass is sold at any of the above sights or at TIX Bay Area in Union Square.

Because the park is so large, the best way to get from one end to the other is by car (though you'll want to do a lot of walking in between). On weekends you can park all day for $3 at the University of California at San Francisco garage (enter at Irving Street and 2nd Avenue); from there a free shuttle leaves every 10 minutes for the park's museums. Muni buses and streetcars also provide service to the park. From May through October free guided walking tours of the park are offered every weekend by the Friends of Recreation and Parks (☎ 415/263–0991). Be forewarned: The fog can sweep into the park with amazing speed; always bring a sweatshirt or jacket.

Sights to See

Asian Art Museum. A distinctive Spanish-style building with an Ottoman-shape fountain in front houses both the Asian and de Young museums. The Asian Art Museum contains a collection of more than 12,000 sculptures, paintings, and ceramics from 40 countries, illustrating major periods of Asian art, mostly Chinese. One standout permanent exhibit is the Leventritt Collection of blue-and-white porcelain. On the second floor are treasures from Iran, Turkey, Syria, India, Tibet, Nepal, Pakistan, Korea, Japan, Afghanistan, and Southeast Asia. Both the de Young and Asian Art museums have daily guided tours. ⊠ *Tea Garden Dr. off John F. Kennedy Dr., near 10th Ave. and Fulton St.,* ☎ *415/668–8921.* ⊑ *$6 for both the Asian and de Young museums (additional $1 for same-day admission to Legion of Honor Museum in Lincoln Park).* ☉ *Wed.–Sun. 9:30–5, 1st Wed. of month until 8:45.*

NEED A
BREAK?

The **Japanese Tea Garden** (☎ 415/752–4227), next to the Asian Art Museum, is a serene 4-acre landscape of small ponds, streams, waterfalls, stone bridges, Japanese sculptures, bonsai trees, miniature pagodas, and some nearly vertical wooden "humpback" bridges—all created for the 1894 Mid-Winter Exposition. The Tea House, a low-lit space with hanging lanterns and long wooden benches where tea and cookies are served, is a popular spot for relaxing.

Beach Chalet. This 1925 chalet overlooking Ocean Beach is one of Willis Polk's simpler designs, yet it still impresses. A wraparound Works Projects Administration mural depicts the city in the 1930s; labels describe the minihistory on the panels. A three-dimensional model of the park, artifacts from the 1894 Mid-Winter Exposition and other park events, and a visitor center are here as well. The brew pub–restaurant upstairs has views of the Farallon Islands 36 mi away. ⊠ *The Great Hwy., just south of Fulton St.*

☾ **California Academy of Sciences.** One of the country's top-five natural history museums, the academy houses an aquarium and a planetarium plus numerous exhibits. The **Steinhart Aquarium,** with its dramatic 100,000-gallon Fish Round-about, is home to thousands of creatures and a living coral reef. The "Touch Tide Pool" allows kids to cozy up to starfish, hermit crabs, and other sea creatures.

The Earthquake Floor in the **Earth and Space Hall** has an "earthquake floor" that allows you to experience simulated temblors at various intensities. In the **Wild California Hall,** a 14,000-gallon aquarium tank shows underwater life at the Farallons (islands off the coast of northern California), life-size elephant-seal models, and video information on the state's wildlife. The innovative **Life Through Time Hall** tells the story of evolution from the beginnings of life on earth through the age of dinosaurs to the age of mammals. One of the best exhibits is **African Hall,** depicting animals (real but stuffed) specific to Africa; don't miss the sights and sounds of the African watering hole at the end of the room.

There is an additional charge (up to $2.50) for **Morrison Planetarium** shows (☏ 415/750–7145 for daily schedule). The Laserium presents evening laser-light shows (☏ 415/750–7138) at Morrison Planetarium, accompanied by rock, classical, and other types of music; educational shows outline laser technology. Around the southeast corner of the building is the **Shakespeare Garden,** with 200 plants mentioned by the Bard, as well as bronze-engraved panels with floral quotations. ⊠ *Music Concourse Dr. off South Dr., across from Asian Art and de Young museums,* ☏ *415/750–7145.* ☎ *$7; $1 discount with Muni transfer; free 1st Wed. of month.* ☉ *Memorial Day–Labor Day, daily 9–6; Labor Day–Memorial Day, daily 10–5.*

Conservatory. The oldest building in the park (built in 1876) and the last remaining wood-frame Victorian conservatory in the country, the Conservatory is a copy of London's famous Kew Gardens. Because of damage from a 1995 storm, the Conservatory is closed indefinitely, but its tropical garden, seasonal displays, and permanent exhibit of rare orchids are still being maintained. ⊠ *Conservatory Dr. near Fulton St.,* ☎ *415/362–0808.*

Dutch Windmill. At the very western end of the park is the 1902 Dutch Windmill, with its patina dome, wood-shingled arms and upper section, and heavy cement bottom. The windmill overlooks the curvy, photogenic **Queen Wilhelmina Tulip Garden,** which blooms in early spring and late summer. ⊠ *Between 47th Ave. and the Great Hwy.*

M. H. de Young Memorial Museum. The de Young contains the best collection of American art on the West Coast, including paintings, sculpture, textiles, and decorative arts from Colonial times through the 20th century. The John D. Rockefeller III Collection of American Paintings is especially noteworthy, with more than 200 paintings of masters such as Copley, Eakins, Bingham, and Sargent. Don't miss the room of landscapes, dominated by Frederic Church's moody, almost psychedelic *Rainy Season in the Tropics,* or the gallery of American still lifes, including the trompe l'oeil paintings of William Harnett. The de Young also has dramatic collections of African and Native American art. Ongoing textile installations showcase everything from tribal clothing to couture. The museum hosts traveling shows—often blockbuster events that draw long lines and additional admission charges. The **Café de Young** has outdoor seating in the lovely Oakes Garden. ⊠ *Tea Garden Dr. off JFK Dr., near 10th Ave. and Fulton St.,* ☎ *415/863–3330 for 24-hr information.* ▱ *$6 for de Young and Asian museums (additional $1 for same-day admission to Legion of Honor Museum in Lincoln Park); free 1st Wed. of month (until 5).* ◷ *Wed.–Sun. 9:30–5, 1st Wed. of month until 8:45.*

Stow Lake. One of the most picturesque spots in Golden Gate Park, this small, serene body of water surrounds Strawberry Hill; a couple of bridges allow you to cross over and ascend the hill (the old 19th-century stone bridge on the southwest side of the lake is especially quaint). A waterfall cascades down from the top of the hill, and panoramic views make it worth the short hike up here. Down below, rent a boat or bicycle (☎ 415/752–0347) or stroll around the perimeter. Just to the left of the waterfall sits the elaborate Chinese Pavilion, a gift from the city of Taipei; it was shipped in 6,000 pieces and assembled on the shore of Strawberry Hill Island in 1981. Stow Lake is a favorite spot for the Russian immigrants who live in the neighborhood just north of the park. ✉ *Just east of Cross Over Dr.*

Strybing Arboretum & Botanical Gardens. You're bound to enjoy this area even if horticulture isn't your thing. The 70-acre arboretum specializes in plants from areas with climates similar to that of the Bay Area, such as the west coast of Australia, South Africa, and the Mediterranean; more than 8,000 plants and tree varieties bloom in gardens throughout the grounds. Informative group walks or children's walks can be arranged (☎ 415/661–3584), and Strybing regularly hosts classes, lectures, and plant sales. A bookstore and an exhaustive reference library is on the grounds. ✉ *9th Ave. at Lincoln Way,* ☎ *415/661–1316.* 🎫 *Free.* ☻ *Weekdays 8–4:30, weekends and holidays 10–5. Tours leave the bookstore weekdays at 1:30, weekends at 10:30.*

Lincoln Park and the Western Shoreline

No other American city provides such close-up viewing of the power and fury of the surf attacking the shore. A different breed of San Franciscan chooses to live in this area: surfers who brave the heaviest fog to ride the waves; writers who seek solace and inspiration in this city outpost; dog lovers committed to giving their pets a good workout each day. It's here you'll feel as if you're truly on the edge of a continent, and it's here that you leave San Francisco behind and enter California, which, as they say, *is* a state of mind.

From Land's End in Lincoln Park you'll have some of the best views of the Golden Gate (the opening of San Francisco Bay, named long before the bridge was built) and the Marin Headlands. Ocean Beach and the Great Highway run along the western edge of the city from just below the Cliff House to the San Francisco Zoo. The wind is often strong along the shoreline, summer fog can blanket the ocean beaches, and the water is cold and usually too rough for swimming. Carry a jacket and bring binoculars.

Sights to See

California Palace of the Legion of Honor. Spectacularly situated on cliffs overlooking the ocean, the Golden Gate Bridge, and the Marin Headlands, this landmark building is a fine repository of European art. A pyramidal glass skylight in the entrance court illuminates the lower-level galleries, which showcase prints and drawings, English and European porcelain, and ancient Assyrian, Greek, Roman, and Egyptian art. The 20-plus galleries on the upper level hold the permanent collection of European art (paintings, sculpture, decorative arts, tapestries) from the 14th through the 20th centuries. The Rodin collection is among the most notable, with two galleries devoted to the master and a third with works by Rodin and other 19th-century sculptors. (An original cast of Rodin's *The Thinker* welcomes you as you walk through the courtyard.)

The **Legion Café,** on the lower level, has a garden terrace. North of the museum (across Camino del Mar) is George Segal's *The Holocaust,* a sobering monument whose white-plaster figures lie sprawled and twisted on the ground, while one lone figure peers out from behind barbed wire. ⊠ *34th Ave. at Clement St.,* ☎ *415/863–3330 for 24-hr information.* ☞ *$7, free 2nd Wed. of month.* ☼ *Tues.–Sun. 9:30–5, 1st Sat. of month until 8:45.*

Cliff House. This San Francisco landmark has had three incarnations. The original, built in 1863, hosted several U.S. presidents and wealthy locals who would drive their carriages out to Ocean Beach; it was destroyed by fire on Christmas Day 1894. The second and most beloved Cliff House was built in 1896; it rose eight stories with an observation tower 200 ft above sea level. It also succumbed to fire a year after surviving the 1906 quake. The present building, erected in 1909, has restaurants, a pub, and a gift shop. The dining areas overlook Seal Rock (the barking marine mammals sunning themselves are actually sea lions).

Just below the Cliff House is the **Musée Mécanique** (☎ 415/386–1170), a time-warped arcade with a collection of antique mechanical contrivances, including peep shows and nickelodeons. Some of the favorites are the giant, rather creepy "Laughing Sal," an arm-wrestling machine, and the many mechanical fortune-telling figures. The museum is open daily; admission is free, but you may want to bring a few quarters or singles to play the many games. ✉ *1090 Point Lobos Ave.,* ☎ *415/386–3330.* ⊙ *Weekdays 8 AM–10:30 PM, weekends 8 AM–11 PM; cocktails served nightly until 2 AM.*

Lincoln Park. At one time all the city's cemeteries were here, segregated by nationality. The caskets were moved to make way for an 18-hole golf course with large Monterey cypresses lining the fairways. There are scenic walks throughout the 275-acre park, with postcard-perfect views, especially from **Land's End** (the trail starts outside the Palace of the Legion of Honor, at the end of El Camino del Mar). The trails out to Land's End, however, are for skilled hikers only: Landslides are frequent, and danger lurks along the steep cliffs. ✉ *Entrance at 34th Ave. at Clement St.*

Ocean Beach. Stretching 3 mi along the western (Pacific) side of the city, this is a beautiful beach for walking, running, or lying in the sun—but not for swimming. Surfers here wear wet suits year-round as the water is extremely cold. Paths on both sides of the Great Highway lead from Lincoln Avenue to Sloat Boulevard (near the zoo); the beachside path winds through landscaped sand dunes, while the paved path across the highway is good for biking and rollerblading. ✉ *Along the Great Highway from the Cliff House to Sloat Blvd. and beyond.*

ॐ **San Francisco Zoo.** First established in 1889 in Golden Gate Park, the zoo is home to more than 130 species of birds and animals designated as endangered. Among the protected are the snow leopard, Sumatran tiger, jaguar, and Asian elephant. A favorite attraction is the greater one-horned rhinocerous, next to the African elephants. Another popular zoo resident is Prince Charles, a rare white tiger and the first of its kind to be exhibited in the West. **Gorilla World** is one of the largest and most natural gorilla habitats of any zoo in the world. The **Primate Discovery Center** houses 14 endangered species in atriumlike enclosures.

The children's zoo has a minipopulation of about 300 mammals, birds, and reptiles, plus an insect zoo, a baby-animal nursery, and a beautifully restored 1921 Dentzel carousel. The **Feline Conservation Center,** a large, naturalistic setting for rare cats, plays a key role in the zoo's efforts to encourage breeding among endangered felines. The new 7-acre **South American Gateway** exhibit re-creates habitats on that continent, replete with howler monkeys, tapirs, and a cloud forest. Don't miss the big cat feeding—they love their horse meat—Tuesday–Sunday at 2. ⊠ *Sloat Blvd. and the Great Hwy.,* ☎ *415/753–7083.* ⊡ *$7; free 1st Wed. of month; children's zoo $1.* ☉ *Daily 10–5; children's zoo weekdays 11–4, weekends 10:30–4:30.*

The Mission District and Noe Valley

The sunny Mission District wins out in San Francisco's unique system of microclimates—it's always the last to succumb to fog. Home to lively Italian and Irish communities earlier in the century—you'll still find Italian restaurants and Irish pubs here, as well as Arabic bookstores, Vietnamese markets, and Filipino eateries. The Mission has had a distinctive Latino flavor since the late 1960s, when immigrants from Mexico and Central America began arriving. Around 24th Street, the heart of the Latino Mission, open-air markets sell huge Mexican papayas and plantains, tiny restaurants serve *sopa de mariscos* (fish soup), and shops proffer religious paraphernalia.

Cinco de Mayo (5th of May) is an important fiesta in the Mission: A weekend of music, dance, and parades commemorates the Mexican victory over French troops in 1862. And come Memorial Day weekend, the revelers come out in earnest, when Carnaval transforms the neighborhood into a northern Rio de Janeiro for three days. Stages for live music and dancers, as well as crafts and food booths, are set up along Harrison Street. The Grand Carnaval Parade, along Mission Street, caps the celebration.

The Mission has seen an influx of a largely white, young, bohemian crowd—political activists, artists and performers, slackers, lesbians and gays—enticed by cheap rents and a burgeoning arts scene. As a result, scads of restaurants, cafés, and shops have sprung up along Valencia, between 16th and 24th streets.

Just uphill from the Mission is Noe Valley, an area that couldn't be more different from its downhill neighbor. The

Mission is chaotic and bustling, culturally diverse and working class; Noe Valley is sedate and slow-paced, largely white and middle class (though decidedly liberal). The neighborhoods are only a few blocks apart, but entirely different worlds. On its western end Noe Valley is just uphill from the predominantly gay Castro neighborhood.

Noe Valley and adjacent Twin Peaks were once known as Rancho San Miguel, a parcel of land given to the last Mexican mayor of San Francisco (then known as Yerba Buena) in 1845. Mayor Don José de Jesús Noe built his ranch house at 22nd and Eureka streets, and the area continued as a bucolic farming community until 1906. But because Noe Valley was so little affected by the quake, many of the displaced settled here. It was predominantly working class (and largely Irish) until the early 1980s, when it saw an influx of well-shod liberals.

Today Noe Valley feels more like a small (though prosperous) town than any other neighborhood in San Francisco. The storefronts are modest, everyone seems to know each other, and the pace is fairly slow; crowds slump in front of 24th Street's bagel shop and nearby coffee shops, and strollers clog the sidewalks. As resident and *Zippy the Pinhead* cartoonist Bill Griffith puts it: "[It's] primarily an urban mall for caffeine addicts and people who have jobs that don't require them to go to an office."

Numbers in the margin correspond to numbers on the Mission District/Noe Valley map.

Sights to See

8 **Axford House.** This mauve house was built when Noe Valley was still a rural area, as evidenced by the hayloft in the gable of the adjacent carriage house. It's surrounded by a well-maintained garden and an attractive iron fence. ⊠ *1190 Noe St., at 25th St.*

6 **Balmy Alley.** Art in the Mission District is not just indoors. In the tradition of the great muralist Diego Rivera, community artists have transformed the walls of their neighborhood. One of the more striking examples is this one-block alley filled with a series of murals. A group of children working with adults started the project in 1971; since then dozens of artists and community workers have steadily added to it, with the aim of promoting peace in Central America, as well as community spirit and AIDS awareness. (Be careful in this area; the other end of the street adjoins the back of a somewhat dangerous housing project.) Two other great murals adorn the rectory building of **St. Peter's Catholic Church**, at 24th and Florida streets, and the **Mission Neighborhood Center**, at the corner of Balmy Alley. ⊠ *24th St. between Harrison and Treat Sts.*

❷ **Creativity Explored.** An atmosphere of joyous, if chaotic, creativity pervades the workshops of this art education center and gallery for developmentally disabled adults. About 70 adults work at the center each day—guided by a staff of 13 artists—making prints, textiles, and ceramics, painting, working in the darkroom, and producing videos. Thirty shows a year are mounted, and the works are shown throughout the world. To see the artists at work, stop by between 10 and 2. ⊠ *3245 16th St.,* ☎ *415/863–2108.* ☉ *Weekdays 9–4:30.*

❺ **Galería de la Raza/Studio 24.** This important showcase for Latino art shows local and international artists and sometimes mounts larger exhibits in conjunction with other Bay Area arts groups. Next door is the nonprofit Studio 24, which sells first-rate prints and paintings by Chicano artists, as well as unique folk art, mainly from Mexico. In early November the studio explodes with art paying tribute to *Dia de los Muertos* (Day of the Dead). In Mexican tradition death is not feared but seen as a part of life—thus the colorful skeleton figurines doing everyday things like housework or playing sports. ⊠ *2857 24th St., at Bryant St.,* ☎ *415/826–8009.* ☉ *Tues.–Sat. noon–6.*

❶ **Mission Dolores.** Mission Dolores encompasses two churches standing side by side. Completed in 1791, the small adobe building known as Mission San Francisco de Asis is the oldest standing structure in San Francisco and the sixth of the 21 missions founded by Father Junípero Serra. Its ceiling depicts original Ohlone Indian basket designs, executed in vegetable dyes. There is a small museum, and the pretty little mission cemetery (made famous by a scene in Alfred Hitchcock's *Vertigo*) maintains the graves of mid-19th-century European immigrants. Today services are held in both the Mission San Francisco de Asis and next door in

The Mission District/Noe Valley

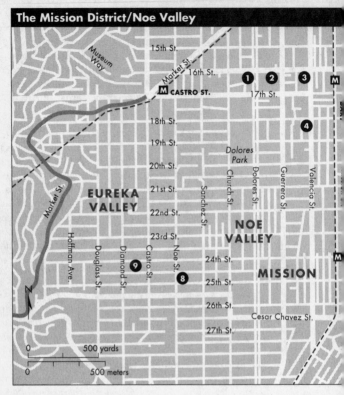

Axford House, **8**
Balmy Alley, **6**
Creativity Explored, **2**
Galería de la Raza/ Studio 24, **5**
Mission Dolores, **1**
Precita Eyes Mural Arts Center, **7**
Roxie Cinema, **3**
Women's Building, **4**

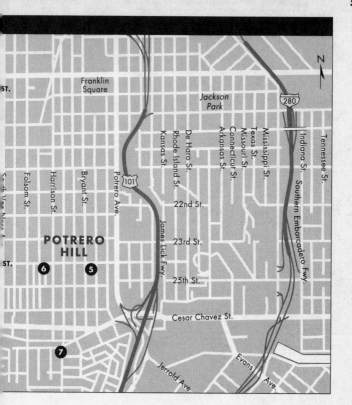

N

ST.

Franklin
Square

Jackson
Park

I-280

ST.

Folsom St.

Harrison St.

Bryant St.

Potrero Ave.

101

De Haro St.
Rhode Island St.
Kansas St.

Arkansas St.
Connecticut St.
Missouri St.
Texas St.
Mississippi St.

Indiana St.
Southern Embarcadero Fwy.

Tennessee St.

22nd St.

**POTRERO
HILL**

James Lick Fwy.

23rd St.

25th St.

ST.

6   5

Cesar Chavez St.

7

Evans Ave.

Jerrold Ave.

the handsome multidomed basilica. ⊠ *Dolores and 16th Sts.*, ☎ *415/621–8203.* 🎫 *$2.* ☉ *Daily 9–4.*

❼ Precita Eyes Mural Arts Center. This nonprofit arts organization gives guided walks of the Mission District's murals. The tours start with a 45-minute slide presentation, and the bus, bike, and walking trips, which take between one and three hours, visit more than 80 murals in the area. May is Mural Awareness Month, with presentations by artists and community celebrations. ⊠ *348 Precita Ave.*, ☎ *415/285– 2287.* 🎫 *$4–$30.* ☉ *Bus and bike tours 3rd Sun. of each month; walks Sat. at 1:30 or daily by appointment.*

NEED A BREAK?   A subdued atmosphere prevails at the homey, yet elegant **Lovejoy's Antiques & Tea Room** (⊠ 1195 Church St., at 24th St., ☎ 415/648–5895), where tables and couches mix in with the antiques for sale. High tea and cream tea are both served, along with traditional English–tearoom "fayre," such as the Ploughman's lunch and sandwiches (oak-smoked finnan haddock is a favorite).

---

❸ Roxie Cinema. The pride of 16th Street is the Roxie Cinema, a consistently solid venue for anything from two-week-long noir festivals to showings of rare concert footage to independent films. ⊠ *3117 16th St.*, ☎ *415/863–1087.* 🎫 *$6.*

❹ Women's Building. The cornerstone of the neighborhood women-owned and -run businesses is the Women's Building, which has held workshops and conferences since 1979. It houses offices for many social and political organizations and sponsors talks and readings by such noted figures as Alice Walker and Angela Davis. The building's striking two-sided exterior mural, depicting women's peacekeeping efforts over the centuries, was completed in September 1994. ⊠ *3543 18th St.*, ☎ *415/431–1180.* ☉ *Weekdays 9–5 (sometimes later, depending on event).*

The Castro

Historians still debate what brought an estimated 100,000 to 250,000 gays and lesbians to the San Francisco area. Some point to the libertarian tradition rooted in Barbary Coast piracy, prostitution, and gambling. Others note that as a huge military embarkation point during World War II, the city was occupied by tens of thousands of mostly single men. Whatever the cause, San Francisco became the city of choice for lesbians and gay men, and Castro Street—nestled at the base of Twin Peaks and just over Buena Vista hill from Haight Street—became its social, cultural, and political center.

Despite the specter of AIDS, the Castro District remains one of the liveliest and most welcoming neighborhoods in the city, especially on weekends. The streets teem with a wide assortment of folks out shopping, pushing political causes, heading to art films, and lingering in bars and cafés. Cutting-edge clothing stores and unique gift shops predominate, as do pairs of pretty young things holding hands.

Numbers in the margin correspond to numbers on the Castro and the Haight map.

Sights to See

★ ❷ **Castro Theatre.** The marquee is the neighborhood's great neon landmark, and the theater itself is the grandest of San Francisco's few remaining movie palaces. Its elaborate Spanish baroque interior is well preserved, and a new pipe organ is played before each nightly showing, ending with a traditional chorus of the Jeanette McDonald standard "San Francisco." The 1,500-capacity crowd can be enthusiastic and vocal, talking back to the screen as loudly as it talks to them. Catch classics, the Fellini film retrospective, or the latest take on same-sex love here. The theater also sponsors the annual **Gay and Lesbian Film Festival** (☎ 415/703–8650), held each June. ⊠ *Castro St. between Market and 18th Sts.,* ☎ *415/621–6120.* ☞ *$6.50.*

❶ **Harvey Milk Plaza.** This plaza, in the spiritual and physical heart of the Castro, is named for the man who electrified the city in 1977 by being elected to its board of supervisors as an openly gay candidate. His high visibility accompanied demands by homosexuals for thorough inclusion in the city's life. San Francisco has responded with a tolerance found nowhere else in the United States: Gay people hold posts throughout local government and are one of the city's strongest voter blocks. Despite rumors to the

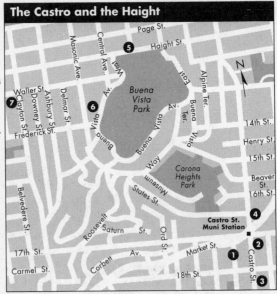

The Castro and the Haight

contrary, the AIDS crisis has barely dampened the Castro's flamboyancy. Gay bars abound around the plaza, and gay-oriented boutiques line Castro, 18th, and Market streets. ⊠ *Castro and Market Sts.*

❸ Hello Gorgeous!! Past video clips, elegant mannequins, and posters of Barbra Streisand, a museum and shop with every conceivable item bearing her likeness awaits you. The proprietor hocked his home to realize this dream of pictures, T-shirts, albums, Barbra's costumes from the films *Yentl* and *The Main Event,* and other objects of obsession. ⊠ *549-A Castro St.,* ☎ *415/864–2628.* 🎟 *$2.50.* 🕒 *Mon.–Thurs. 11–7, Fri.–Sat. 11–8, Sun. 11–6.*

❹ Names Project. Open to anyone who wishes to work on a panel, the Names Project has created a gigantic quilt made of more than 44,000 hand-sewn and -decorated panels, pieced together by loved ones to serve as a memorial to those who have died of AIDS. People come from all over the country to work in this storefront as a labor of love and grief; others send panels here by mail. New additions to the quilt are always on display. ⊠ *2362 Market St.,* ☎ *415/863–1966.* ☉ *Daily noon–5; quilting bee every Wed. 7* PM*–10* PM.

The Haight

East of Golden Gate Park is the neighborhood known as "the Haight." Despite the presence of a Gap store (on the corner of Haight and Ashbury streets, no less) and a growing number of upscale galleries and shops, this is still home to a wandering tribe of Deadheads, with anarchist book collectives and shops selling incense and tie-dyed T-shirts.

Once home to middle-class families of European immigrants, the Haight began to change during the late 1950s and early 1960s when families fled to the suburbs. The big old Victorians deteriorated or were divided into cheap housing. Young people found the neighborhood an affordable and exciting community in which they could live according to new precepts. By 1966 the Haight had become a hot spot for rock bands such as the Grateful Dead—whose members moved into a big Victorian at 710 Ashbury Street—and Jefferson Airplane, whose grand mansion was at 2400 Fulton Street. By 1967, 200,000 young people with "flowers in their hair" and peace and civil rights on their minds were heading for the Haight.

Sharing the continuing fascination with events of the 1960s, many visitors to San Francisco want to see the setting of the Summer of Love. Back in 1967 Gray Lines instituted their "Hippie-Hop," advertising it as "the only foreign tour within the continental limits of the United States," piloted by a driver "especially trained in the sociological significance of the Haight." Today you can find several groups that offer "Summer of Love" tours—some are worth your dime, others aren't.

The Haight's famous political spirit—it was the first neighborhood in the United States to lead a freeway revolt, and it continues to host regular boycotts against chain stores—exists alongside some of the finest Victorian-lined streets in the city. The area is also known for its vintage merchandise, including clothes, records, books, and a host of miscellany, such as crystals, jewelry, and candles.

Numbers in the margin correspond to numbers on the Castro and the Haight map.

Sights to See

⑤ Buena Vista Park. Great city views can be had from this eucalyptus-filled park. Although it's not exactly sedate (drug deals are common), it's a very pretty park, especially on a sunny day. Don't wander here after dark. ⊠ *Haight St. between Lyon St. and Buena Vista Ave. W.*

⑦ Red Victorian Peace Center Bed & Breakfast. You can almost smell the patchouli as you step inside the warm, hippie-dippie atmosphere of the Red Vic B&B. There's a comfy breakfast room and the Peace Center shop downstairs. Eighteen dimly lit rooms are for rent upstairs; the most elaborate is the "Peacock Suite," festooned with peacock feathers, tapestries, stained glass, and figurines. Rooms run from $76 to $200 per night. ⊠ *1665 Haight St.,* ☎ *415/864–1978.*

⑥ Spreckels Mansion. Not to be confused with the Spreckels Mansion of Pacific Heights, this house was built for sugar baron Richard Spreckels in 1887; later tenants included Jack London and Ambrose Bierce. The boxy, putty-color Victorian is in mint condition, with a pretty garden around the front and a series of delicate trellis arches over the driveway. It's a private residence, so admire from afar. ⊠ *737 Buena Vista Ave. W.*

3 Dining

SAN FRANCISCO PROBABLY HAS MORE
restaurants per capita than any other
city in the United States, including New
By Sharon York. Practically every ethnic cuisine is represented. Since
Silva selecting some 100 recommended restaurants is a next-to-
impossible task, we have chosen instead cream-of-the-crop
restaurants to represent each popular style of dining in
various price ranges, in most cases because of the superi-
ority of the food but in some instances because of the view
or ambience.

Because we have focused on those areas of town most fre-
quented by visitors, this meant leaving out some great
places in outlying districts such as the Mission, the Haight,
the Sunset, and the Richmond. The outlying restaurants that
are recommended were chosen because they offer an experience not available elsewhere. All listed restaurants serve
lunch and dinner unless otherwise specified; restaurants are
not open for breakfast unless the morning meal is specifi-
cally mentioned.

Most upper-end restaurants offer valet parking—worth
considering in especially crowded neighborhoods such as
North Beach, Union Square, Nob Hill, the Richmond District, and the Civic Center. There is often a nominal charge
and a time-length restriction on validated parking.

Smoking is banned in most Bay Area restaurants and many
bars, although a number of lounges for cigar smokers have
recently opened. Restaurants do change their policies about
hours, credit cards, and the like. It is always best to make
inquiries in advance.

The price ranges listed below are for an average three-
course meal. Price categories are as follows:

CATEGORY	COST*
$$$$	over $50
$$$	$30–$50
$$	$20–$30
$	under $20

*per person for a three-course meal, excluding drinks, ser-
vice, and 8.5% sales tax

American

Before the 1980s it was hard to find a decent "American" restaurant in the Bay Area. In recent years, however, the offerings have grown and diversified, with fare that includes everything from barbecue to all-American diner food to that mix of Mediterranean-Asian-Latino known as California cuisine, which has become increasingly popular.

Castro

$$ ✕ **2223.** This upper Market Street establishment opened to instant success. Thin-crust pizza topped with pancetta and Teleme cheese, earthy seasonal soups, chicken with garlic-mashed potatoes, and Thai shrimp salad with sesame are among the kitchen's best dishes. Sunday brunch is popular, too. You need a strong pair of lungs here, as the restaurant's crowds and absence of sound buffers make conversation difficult. ✉ *2223 Market St.,* ☎ *415/431–0692. MC, V. No lunch Sat.*

Civic Center

$$$ ✕ **Stars.** This is the culinary temple of Jeremiah Tower, the
★ superchef who claims to have invented California cuisine. Stars is a must on every traveling gourmet's itinerary; it's also where many of the local movers and shakers hang out and a popular place for post-theater dining. The dining room has a clublike ambience, and the food ranges from grills to ragouts to sautés—some daringly creative and some classical. Dinners here are pricey, but those on a budget can order a hot dog, pizza, or stylish chicken tacos at the bar. ✉ *150 Redwood Alley, at Van Ness Ave.,* ☎ *415/861–7827. Reservations essential. AE, DC, MC, V. No lunch weekends.*

$$ ✕ **Carta.** The defining idea here is a difficult one to carry off: a different menu from a different country or region every month; but Carta makes it work beautifully. The talented chefs travel to an eclectic assortment of destinations: Oaxaca, Turkey, Russia, Provence, Morocco, and New England, to name just a few. There are usually about 10 small plates, three main courses, and three desserts. The dining room is small, imaginatively turned out, and comfortable. ✉ *1772 Market St.,* ☎ *415/863–3516. AE, MC, V. Closed Mon. No lunch weekends.*

68

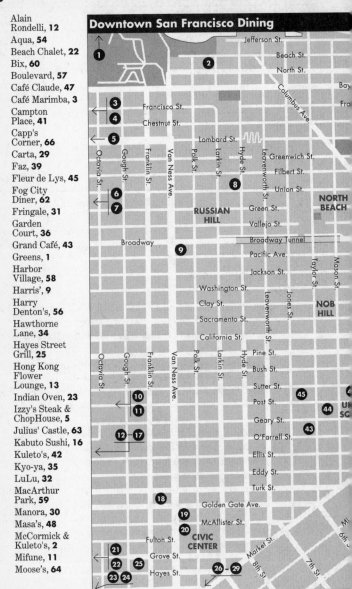

Downtown San Francisco Dining

$$ ✕ **Stars Cafe.** This casual café offers a taste of Jeremiah Tower's renowned Stars cuisine at more down-to-earth prices. Both bar and table seating are available, and although the food too often fluctuates in quality, the convenient location—in the heart of the city's classical music quarter—makes it a regular stop for culture hounds. Trademark items are pizzas from the wood-burning oven and decadent desserts. ✉ *500 Van Ness Ave.,* ☎ *415/861-4344. AE, DC, MC, V.*

Cow Hollow/Marina

$$ ✕ **Perry's.** The West Coast equivalent of P. J. Clarke's in Manhattan, this popular watering hole for the button-down singles set serves good, honest saloon food—London broil, corned beef hash, one of the best hamburgers in town, and a great breakfast. Brunch is served on weekends. A second location, Perry's Downtown, serves the same signature burger and other Perry's standards in a clubby, mahogany-lined space. ✉ *1944 Union St.,* ☎ *415/922–9022;* ✉ *185 Sutter St.,* ☎ *415/989–6895. AE, MC, V.*

Embarcadero North

$$ ✕ **Fog City Diner.** San Francisco's obsession with diners began at Fog City—and its popularity knows no end, despite reports of inconsistent service. The long, narrow dining room emulates a luxurious railroad car, with dark wood paneling, huge windows, and comfortable booths. The menu is innovative, drawing its inspiration from regional cooking throughout the United States. The shareable "small plates" are a fun way to go. ✉ *1300 Battery St.,* ☎ *415/982–2000. D, DC, MC, V.*

$$ ✕ **MacArthur Park.** Year after year San Franciscans pronounce this handsomely renovated pre-earthquake warehouse their favorite spot for ribs, but the oak-wood smoker and mesquite grill also turn out great all-American fare, from steaks and hamburgers to seafood. Takeout is also available. ✉ *607 Front St.,* ☎ *415/398–5700. AE, DC, MC, V. No lunch weekends.*

Embarcadero South

$$–$$$ ✕ **Boulevard.** Two of San Francisco's top restaurant talents are responsible for this highly successful eatery in a magnificent landmark building: Nationally acclaimed chef Nancy Oakes and design partner Pat Kuleto. The setting

In case you want to see the world.

At American Express, we're here to make your journey a smooth one. So we have over 1,700 travel service locations in over 120 countries ready to help. What else would you expect from the world's largest travel agency?

do more ®

AMERICAN EXPRESS

http://www.americanexpress.com/travel

Travel

In case you want to be welcomed there.

We're here to see that you're always welcomed at establishments everywhere. That's why millions of people carry the American Express® Card – for peace of mind, confidence, and security, around the world or just around the corner.

do more ®

In case you're running low.

We're here to help with more than 118,000 Express Cash
locations around the world. In order to enroll, just
call American Express before you start
your vacation.

do more

And just in case.

We're here with American Express® Travelers Cheques and Cheques *for Two.*® They're the safest way to carry money on your vacation and the surest way to get a refund, practically anywhere, anytime.
Another way we help you...

do more.

AMERICAN
EXPRESS

Travelers Cheques

is the 1889 Audiffred Building, a Parisian look-alike that survived the 1906 earthquake and fire. Oakes's menu is seasonally in flux, but you can always count on her signature juxtaposition of rare delicacies such as foie gras with homey comfort foods like maple-cured pork loin. If you can't find or afford a table during regular hours, Boulevard offers a less formal weekday afternoon bistro service. ⊠ *1 Mission St.,* ☎ *415/543–6084. Reservations essential. AE, D, DC, MC, V. No lunch weekends.*

$$ ╳ **Harry Denton's.** Every night's a party at this madcap waterfront hangout, where singles congregate in a Barbary Coast–style bar, and the rugs are rolled up at 10:30 on Thursday, Friday, and Saturday nights for dancing. Sometimes Harry himself—the city's best-known saloon keeper—dances on the bar. At lunchtime the place is quieter, attracting diners with its fine bay view and earthy menu that offers everything from pizza to pasta with baked oysters, pot roast, and burgers. Breakfast is served daily and extends to brunch on weekends. ⊠ *161 Steuart St.,* ☎ *415/882–1333. AE, DC, MC, V.*

Financial District

$$$ ╳ **Rubicon.** With investors like Robin Williams, Robert De Niro, and Francis Ford Coppola, this sleek cherrywood lined restaurant was fated to be a destination, if only for the chance to steal a glance at one of its stars. Set in a stately stone building dating from 1908, Rubicon has the dignified air of a men's club in the downstairs dining room and a somewhat less appealing atmosphere in the ascetic upstairs space. The excellent fare, primarily sophisticated renditions of seafood and poultry, is served on both floors to big shots and common folk, too. ⊠ *558 Sacramento St.,* ☎ *415/434–4100. AE, MC, V. Closed Sun. No lunch Sat.*

North Beach

$$ ╳ **Bix.** In a historic building that was an assay office in gold rush days, this old-fashioned supper club is reminiscent of a theater, with a bustling bar and dining tables downstairs and banquettes on the balcony. Opt for the lower level; the acoustics upstairs are dreadful. The menu offers contemporary renditions of classic American fare; there's piano music in the evenings. ⊠ *56 Gold St.,* ☎ *415/433–6300. AE, D, DC, MC, V. No lunch weekends.*

South of Market

$$$ ✕ **Hawthorne Lane.** Among the booming bevy of SoMa
★ eateries is this popular establishment near the Moscone Cen-
ter. In the large, high-ceiling bar there's a selection of irre-
sistible small plates—Thai-style squid, skewers of grilled
chicken, tempura-battered green beans with mustard sauce,
and stylish pizzas. Patrons in the light-flooded dining room
engage in more serious eating, from foie gras to grilled quail,
all turned out with Mediterranean and Asian touches. ⊠
22 Hawthorne St., ☎ *415/777–9779. Reservations es-
sential. D, DC, MC, V. No lunch weekends.*

Sunset District

$$ ✕ **Beach Chalet.** In a historic colonnaded building with handsome Works Projects Administration–produced murals (☞
Golden Gate Park *in* Chapter 2), this newcomer is *the*
place to watch the sun set over the Pacific while indulging
in fine house-made microbrews and American food. The
beers run the gamut from a light pilsner to Playland pale
ale. The food is an eclectic mix of steamed mussels and
pizzette, house-made chorizo and seafood gumbo. It's a 40-
minute ride on the N Judah streetcar from downtown—
and well worth the trip. ⊠ *1000 Great Hwy.,* ☎
415/386–8439. MC, V.

Union Square

$$$–$$$$ ✕ **Postrio.** Superchef and owner Wolfgang Puck periodically
★ commutes from Los Angeles to make an appearance in the
restaurant's open kitchen. A stunning three-level bar and din-
ing area is highlighted by palm trees and museum-quality
contemporary paintings. Attire is formal; food is Puckish
Californian with Mediterranean and Asian overtones, em-
phasizing pastas, grilled seafood, and house-baked breads.
Substantial breakfast and bar menus (with great pizza) can
be found here as well. ⊠ *545 Post St.,* ☎ *415/776–7825.
Reservations essential. AE, D, DC, MC, V.*

$$$ ✕ **Campton Place.** This ultrasophisticated small hotel put
★ new American cooking on the local culinary map. Chef Todd
Humphries carries on the innovative traditions of opening
chef Bradley Ogden with great aplomb and has embel-
lished traditional American dishes with ethnic flavors. Sample a fuller range of Humphries's culinary accomplishments
with the six-course tasting menu, which stretches from

caviar to squab. Be forewarned that his sunny yellow, delightfully crumbly cornbread can be addictive. Breakfast and brunch are major events. A bar menu offers samplings of appetizers plus a caviar extravaganza. ✉ *340 Stockton St.,* ☎ *415/955–5555. Reservations essential. AE, D, DC, MC, V.*

$$ ✕ Grand Café. This Beaux Arts establishment, inside the Hotel Monaco at the center of the theater district, draws people for everything from its early morning breakfast to its late-night bar menu. The menus for the main dining room and the more casual bar area are French-Californian, with an emphasis on seasonal local ingredients. The dramatic dining room, formerly a ballroom, is decorated with eight cabaret-style murals, fanciful sculptures of human figures, striking chandeliers, and large, comfortable booths. ✉ *Hotel Monaco, 501 Geary St.,* ☎ *415/292–0101. AE, D, DC, MC, V.*

$$ ✕ Rumpus. With Caesar salad, burgers, club sandwiches, and New York steak at lunchtime, this casual bistro has a true American menu. The comfortable space on an old-time alley in the heart of downtown offers a bar menu all day long and late into the night. ✉ *1 Tillman Pl., at Grant Ave.,* ☎ *415/421–2300. AE, MC, V.*

Chinese

For nearly a century Chinese restaurants in San Francisco were confined to Chinatown, and the cooking was largely an Americanized version of peasant-style Cantonese. The past few decades, however, have seen an influx of restaurants representing the wide spectrum of Chinese cuisine: the subtly seasoned fare of Canton; the hot and spicy cooking of Hunan and Szechuan; the meats, steamed buns, and braised freshwater fish of Shanghai; and the northern style of Beijing, where meat and dumplings replace seafood and rice as staples—as well as the seldom-encountered cooking of the Hakkas, a southern Chinese people known for their country fare. For some years now the scene has been influenced by the high style of Hong Kong.

Chinatown

$–$$ ✕ **R&G Lounge.** The name conjures up an image of a dark bar, but the two-floor restaurant is actually as bright as a new penny. Downstairs is a no-tablecloth dining room that is always packed. The classier upstairs space (entrance on Commercial Street), complete with shoji-lined private rooms, is a favorite stop for Chinese businessmen and anyone seeking exceptional Cantonese banquet fare. A menu with photographs helps diners decide among the many exotic dishes, from dried scallops with seasonal vegetables to steamed bean curd with shrimp meat. ⊠ *631 Kearny St.,* ☎ *415/982–7877 or 415/982–3811. AE, DC, MC, V.*

Embarcadero North

$$ ✕ **Harbor Village.** Classic Cantonese cooking, dim sum lunches, and fresh seafood from its own tanks are the hallmarks of this 400-seat branch of a Hong Kong establishment, which sent five of its master chefs to supervise the initial organization of the kitchen. The setting is opulent, with Chinese antiques and teak furnishings, and the main dining room is usually crowded with business tycoons and three-generation families. A gallery of private rooms harbors large banquet tables perfect for celebrating any special occasion. There's validated parking at the Embarcadero Center Garage. ⊠ *4 Embarcadero Center,* ☎ *415/781–8833. AE, DC, MC, V.*

Financial District

$ ✕ **Yank Sing.** The city's oldest teahouse is still considered by many to be the best purveyor of midday Cantonese dim sum. The kitchen offers some five dozen or so varieties of the little morsels on a rotating basis. The Battery Street location seats 300, while the older Stevenson Street site is far smaller, a cozy refuge for Market Street office workers who fuel up on steamed buns and parchment chicken at lunchtime. ⊠ *427 Battery St.,* ☎ *415/362–1640;* ⊠ *49 Stevenson St., at Market St.,* ☎ *415/541–4949. AE, DC, MC, V. Stevenson branch closed weekends. No dinner.*

Richmond District

$$ ✕ **Hong Kong Flower Lounge.** High-quality Cantonese cuisine is the focus at this attractive establishment. The kitchen is known in particular for its seafood—crabs, shrimp, catfish, lobsters, scallops—which is plucked straight from tanks and prepared in a variety of ways, from classic to contemporary. Chefs here are famous for keeping up with whatever is currently hot in Hong Kong eateries. Check the prices before you order, as these denizens of the deep can be costly. Midday dim sum is available. ⊠ *5322 Geary Blvd.,* ☎ *415/668–8998. AE, D, DC, MC, V.*

$–$$ ✕ **Ton Kiang.** The lightly seasoned Hakka cuisine, rarely found in this country, was introduced to San Francisco at this restaurant, with salt-baked chicken, braised stuffed bean curd, wine-flavored dishes, delicate fish and beef balls, and casseroles of meat and seafood cooked in clay pots. Don't overlook the seafood—salt-and-pepper squid or shrimp, braised catfish, or stir-fried crab, for example. Of the two branches on Geary Boulevard, the newer, at 5821, is more stylish and serves excellent dim sum that many aficionados consider the best in the city. ⊠ *3148 Geary Blvd.,* ☎ *415/752–4440;* ⊠ *5821 Geary Blvd.,* ☎ *415/387–8273. MC, V.*

French

A renaissance of the classic haute cuisine occurred during the 1960s, but in the early '90s a number of French restaurants closed. Nouvelle cuisine came and went, and now the big draw is the bistro or brasserie, featuring a light, contemporary style of cooking.

Embarcadero North

$$ ✕ **Pastis.** At lunchtime the sunny cement bar and sleek wooden banquettes here are crowded with workers from the surrounding neighborhood offices; they come to fuel up on steamed salmon with celery root or grilled prawns marinated in *pastis* (anise-flavored French liqueur). The evening menu may include seared scallops, braised oxtails, or duck confit. This is chef-owner Gerald Hirigoyen's newest venture, a popular successor to his renowned South of Market bistro Fringale (☞ *below*), and a worthy addition to the city's Gallic restaurant roster. ⊠ *1015 Battery St.,* ☎ *415/391–2555. AE, MC, V. Closed Sun. No lunch Sat.*

Financial District

$ ✕ **Café Claude.** At this standout French bistro near Notre Dame des Victoires Catholic church and the French consulate, you'll find a zinc bar, old-fashioned banquettes, and cinema posters that once actually outfitted a little bar in the City of Light's 11th arrondissement. Order a croque monsieur or salade niçoise from the French-speaking staff, and you might forget what country you're in. Order a pastis, and you'll soon be whistling the "Marseillaise." ⊠ *7 Claude La.,* ☏ *415/392–3505. AE, DC, MC, V. Closed Sun.*

Nob Hill

$$$–$$$$ ✕ **Ritz-Carlton Dining Room and Terrace.** This neoclassic
★ showplace's Dining Room is formal and elegant and has a harpist playing; it serves only three- to five-course dinners, priced by the course, not by the item. The Terrace, a cheerful, informal spot with a large garden patio, serves breakfast, lunch, dinner, and a Sunday jazz brunch, with piano music at lunchtime and a jazz trio at weekend dinners. The Dining Room turns out an urbane French menu with Bay Area touches, and the Terrace offers a more casual, French-California menu. ⊠ *600 Stockton St.,* ☏ *415/296–7465. AE, D, DC, MC, V. Closed Sun. No lunch.*

Richmond District

$$–$$$ ✕ **Alain Rondelli.** Hailed as one of France's top young
★ chefs, Paris-born Alain Rondelli owns this beguiling little restaurant in a storefront. The cuisine utilizes his background in classic-yet-contemporary French cooking and adapts it to the agricultural abundance and Asian-Hispanic influences of California: a zap of jalapeño chili here, a bit of star anise there. Two-part entrées are a Rondelli signature: a breast of chicken followed with a confit of the leg in a custard tart, for example. Desserts range from homey to exquisite. ⊠ *126 Clement St.,* ☏ *415/387–0408. MC, V. Closed Mon.–Tues.*

South of Market

$$ ✕ **Fringale.** The bright yellow paint on this dazzling bistro
★ stands out like a beacon on an otherwise bleak industrial street, attracting a Pacific Heights–Montgomery Street clientele. They come for the French Basque–inspired cre-

ations of Biarritz-born chef Gerald Hirigoyen, whose classic *frisée aux lardons* (grilled scallops), and crème brûlée are hallmarks. ⊠ *570 4th St.,* ☎ *415/543–0573. Reservations essential. AE, MC, V. Closed Sun. No lunch Sat.*

Union Square

$$$$ ✕ **Fleur de Lys.** The creative cooking of French chef Hubert Keller has brought every conceivable culinary award to this romantic spot that some consider the best French restaurant in town. The menu changes constantly, but lobster bisque, Maryland crab cakes, seared venison medallions, and veal on a bed of wild mushrooms are regular features of the Keller repertoire. The intimate dining room, like a sheikh's tent, is encased with hundreds of yards of paisley. ⊠ *777 Sutter St.,* ☎ *415/673–7779. Reservations essential. Jacket required. AE, DC, MC, V. Closed Sun. and most major holidays.*

$$$$ ✕ **Masa's.** Presentation is as important as the food itself
★ in this pretty, flower-filled dining spot in the Vintage Court Hotel. Chef Julian Serrano carries on the tradition of the late Masa Kobayashi. In fact, some Masa regulars say his cooking is even better. Decadent ingredients such as foie gras and black truffles figure largely on the menu. Try the savory napoleon of alternating slices of potato and lobster doused in a saffron dressing or any of the savory first-course tarts. ⊠ *648 Bush St.,* ☎ *415/989–7154. Reservations essential. Jacket and tie. AE, D, DC, MC, V. Closed Sun.–Mon. and 1st 2 wks of Jan. No lunch.*

Greek and Middle Eastern

The foods of Greece and the Middle East have much in common: a preponderance of lamb and eggplant dishes, a widespread use of phyllo pastry, and an abundance of pilaf. A handful of restaurants around town offer Hellenic flavors.

Financial District

$$ ✕ **Faz.** This lovely second-story ocher dining room is devoted to food from both sides of the Mediterranean. Start with eastern-inspired appetizers such as creamy *baba ghanoush* (eggplant spread); beef-and-rice-filled dolmas; or a Persian-inspired platter of feta cheese, pungent olives, and garden-fresh herbs. Then move on to pastas and pizzas that

celebrate the robust foods of the west. Be sure to order the signature house-smoked fish platter, which includes salmon, trout, and sometimes sturgeon. ⊠ *161 Sutter St.,* ☎ *415/362–0404. AE, DC, MC, V. Closed Sun. No lunch Sat.*

Sunset District

$ ✕ **Stoyanof's Cafe.** This light-filled Greek outpost, with an outdoor seating area that beckons on sunny days, offers large healthful salads, various phyllo-wrapped savories and sweets, kebabs, sandwiches, and other plates that conjure up balmy breezes blowing off the Aegean. The restaurant lies just steps beyond the southern border of Golden Gate Park, making it a good place to stop after a tour of the nearby Strybing Arboretum or Academy of Sciences. ⊠ *1240 9th Ave.,* ☎ *415/664–3664. MC, V. Closed Mon.*

Indian

Most of San Francisco's Indian restaurants specialize in the cuisine of northern India, which is more subtly seasoned and not as hot as its southern counterparts. At these restaurants you'll find succulent meats and crispy breads from the clay-lined tandoori oven.

The Haight

$$ ✕ **Indian Oven.** The tandoori chef at this handsome, cozy Victorian storefront restaurant has mastered the intricacies of cooking in northern India's classic clay oven, consistently turning out flavorful meats and breads for the steady flow of subcontinental food aficionados. There's an excellent roasted eggplant dish; and the chicken curries and crisp vegetable *pakoras* (fritters), served with a sprightly tamarind chutney, are another good bet. A complete meal, called a *thali* for the metal plate on which it is served, includes a choice of entrée, plus soup, a curried vegetable, cardamom-scented basmati rice, nan, and chutney. ⊠ *223 Fillmore St.,* ☎ *415/626–1628. MC, V. No lunch.*

Italian

Italian food in San Francisco spans the "boot" from the mild cooking of northern Italy to the tomato-rich cuisine of the south. Most distinctive is the style indigenous to San Francisco, known as North Beach Italian—such dishes as cioppino (a fisherman's stew) and Joe's special (a mélange of eggs, spinach, and ground beef).

Civic Center

$$$ ✕ **Vivande Ristorante.** The newest ristorante of owner-chef Carlo Middione, a highly regarded authority on the food of southern Italy, features rustic fare, from focaccia with grilled radicchio and fennel to pasta tossed with a tangle of mushrooms to grilled lamb chops. The spacious room is welcoming, and a late-supper menu finds music lovers regularly grabbing a bite after nearby performances. ⊠ *670 Golden Gate Ave.,* ☏ *415/673–9245. AE, DC, MC, V.*

Cow Hollow/Marina

$$ ✕ **Pane e Vino.** It's no easy task to snag a table in this Cow
★ Hollow trattoria, where roasted whole sea bass, creamy risotto, and pastas tossed with sprightly tomato sauces are among the dishes the legion of regulars can't resist. The Italian-born owner-chef concentrates on specialties from Tuscany and the north, dishing them up in a charming room decorated with rustic wooden furniture and bright white walls punctuated with colorful pottery. ⊠ *3011 Steiner St.,* ☏ *415/346–2111. MC, V. No lunch Sun.*

North Beach

$$$ ✕ **Julius' Castle.** The view from this legendary Telegraph Hill restaurant is arguably the best in the city: You can see both bridges, Treasure Island, Alcatraz, and the East Bay hills. For decades the menu was no match for the panorama, but in the mid-'90s the kitchen took a favorable Italian turn, and diners have since been treated to pricey fare that, although not extraordinary, is considerably improved. The grilled salmon fillet with fava beans and caramelized onions is a good choice, as is the pheasant with seared polenta. Professional service adds to the experience. ⊠ *1541 Montgomery St.,* ☏ *415/392–2222. Reservations essential. AE, DC, MC, V. No lunch.*

$$ ✕ **Rose Pistola.** The name honors one of North Beach's
★ most revered barkeeps, and the food celebrates the neighborhood's Ligurian roots. A wide assortment of small antipasti plates—roasted peppers, house-cured fish, fava beans, and pecorino cheese—and pizzas from the wood-

burning oven are favorites, as are the classic San Francisco seafood stew called cioppino, and roasted rabbit with polenta. A large bar area opens onto the sidewalk, and an immense exhibition kitchen lets customers keep an eye on their orders. ⊠ *532 Columbus Ave.,* ☎ *415/399–0499. Reservations essential. AE, MC, V.*

$ ✕ **Capp's Corner.** At one of the last family-style trattorias,
★ diners sit elbow to elbow at long oilcloth-covered tables to feast on bountiful, well-prepared five-course dinners. For calorie counters or the budget-minded, a simpler option includes a tureen of minestrone, salad, and pasta. ⊠ *1600 Powell St.,* ☎ *415/989–2589. AE, D, DC, MC, V. No lunch weekends.*

Union Square

$$ ✕ **Kuleto's.** The contemporary cooking of northern Italy,
★ the atmosphere of old San Francisco, and a terrific bar menu of antipasti have made this spot a hit since the 1980s. It takes its name from renowned restaurant designer Pat Kuleto, whose artistic hand is evident throughout the Bay Area. Publike booths and a long, open kitchen fill one side of the restaurant; a gardenlike, skylighted room lies beyond. Grilled seafood dishes are among the specialties. Breakfast is also served. ⊠ *221 Powell St.,* ☎ *415/397–7720. AE, D, DC, MC, V.*

$$ ✕ **Scala's Bistro.** Smart leather-and-wood booths, an extravagant mural, and an appealing menu make this one of downtown's most attractive destinations. A large open kitchen stands at the rear of the fashionable dining room, where regulars and out-of-town visitors sit down to breakfast, lunch, and dinner. Grilled Portobello mushrooms and a tower of fried calamari are among the favorite antipasti, while the pastas and grilled meats satisfy most main-course appetites. ⊠ *432 Powell St.,* ☎ *415/395–8555. AE, DC, MC, V.*

Japanese

Japanese menus usually embrace a number of different types of cooking: *yaki* (marinated and grilled foods), tempura, *udon* and *soba* (noodle dishes), *donburi* (meats and vegetables served over rice), and *nabemono* (meals cooked in one pot, often at the table). Sushi bars are extremely popular in San Francisco; most offer a selection of sushi (vinegared rice with fish or vegetables) and sashimi (raw fish). Tatami seating means sitting on mats at low tables.

Financial District

$$–$$$
★
✕ **Kyo-ya.** Refined Japanese dining has been introduced with extraordinary authenticity at this showplace within the Palace Hotel. In Japan a *kyo-ya* is a nonspecialized restaurant that serves a wide range of food. Here, the range is spectacular, encompassing tempuras, one-pot dishes, deep-fried and grilled meats, and three dozen sushi selections. The lunch menu is more limited than dinner but does include a *shokado,* a sampler of four dishes encased in a handsome lacquered box. ⊠ *Palace Hotel, 2 New Montgomery St., at Market St.,* ☎ *415/546–5000. AE, D, DC, MC, V. Closed Sun. No lunch Mon. and Sat.*

Japantown

$
✕ **Mifune.** Thin, brown soba (buckwheat) and thick, white udon (wheat) are the specialties at this outpost of an Osaka-based noodle empire. A line often snakes out the door, but the house-made noodles, served both hot and cold and with more than a score of toppings, are worth the wait. Diners slurp down big bowls of traditional Japanese combinations like fish cake–crowned udon and *tenzaru* (cold noodles and hot tempura with a gingery dipping sauce). Validated parking is available at the Japan Center garage. ⊠ *Japan Center, Kintetsu Building, 1737 Post St.,* ☎ *415/922–0337. Reservations not accepted. AE, D, DC, MC, V.*

$
✕ **Sanppo.** This small place has an enormous selection: yakis, nabemono dishes, donburi, udon, and soba, not to mention featherlight tempura, interesting side dishes, and sushi. Ask for validated parking at the Japan Center garage. ⊠ *1702 Post St.,* ☎ *415/346–3486. Reservations not accepted. MC, V. Closed Mon. No lunch Sun.*

Richmond District

$$
✕ **Kabuto Sushi.** For one of the most spectacular acts in town, head out Geary Boulevard past Japantown to tiny Kabuto, and watch master chef Sachio Kojima flash his knives with the grace of a samurai warrior. In addition to exceptional sushi and sashimi, traditional Japanese dinners

are served in the dining room. For an authentic experience, request tatami seating in the shoji-screened area. ⊠ *5116 Geary Blvd.,* ☎ *415/752–5652. MC, V. Closed Sun.–Mon. No lunch.*

Mediterranean

In its climate and topography, its agriculture and viticulture, and the orientation of many of its early settlers, northern California resembles the Mediterranean region. "Mediterranean" restaurants primarily offer a mix of southern French and northern Italian food, but some include accents from Spain, Greece, and more distant ports of call.

Civic Center

$$–$$$ ✕ **Zuni Café & Grill.** Zuni's Italian-Mediterranean menu and
★   its unpretentious atmosphere pack in the crowds from early morning to late evening. A spacious, window-filled balcony dining area overlooks the large bar, where shellfish, one of the best oyster selections in town, and drinks are dispensed. A whole roast chicken and Tuscan bread salad for two is a popular order here, as are the grilled meats and vegetables. Even the hamburgers are topped with Gorgonzola and served on herbed focaccia. Accompany one with the addictive shoestring potatoes. ⊠ *1658 Market St.,* ☎ *415/552–2522. Reservations essential. AE, MC, V. Closed Mon.*

Cow Hollow/Marina

$$–$$$ ✕ **PlumpJack Café.** This clubby dining room, with its
★   smartly attired clientele, takes its name from an opera composed by oil tycoon and music lover Gordon Getty, whose sons are two of the partners here. The regularly changing menu spans the Mediterranean, with an herbed chicken flanked by polenta and crispy duck confit among the possibilities. The café is an offshoot of the nearby highly regarded wine shop of the same name, which stocks the café with some of the best-price vintages in town. ⊠ *3201 Fillmore St.,* ☎ *415/463–4755. AE, MC, V. Closed Sun. No lunch Sat.*

Financial District

$$$ ✕ **Vertigo.** Arguably San Francisco's most famous building, the Transamerica Pyramid is also home to one of the city's

most stunning restaurants. The three-tiered space has see-through ceilings, a parklike entrance, and an inviting French and Italian menu with a strong Asian accent: A grilled pork chop arrives with curry-dusted beans, while risotto is flavored with lime. Seafood is especially fresh here—and like everything else, it's creatively prepared. A bar menu offers afternoon snacks. ⊠ *600 Montgomery St.,* ☎ *415/433–7250. AE, D, DC, MC, V. Closed Sun. No lunch Sat.*

North Beach

$$ ✕ **Moose's.** Longtime restaurateur Ed Moose's latest celebrity hangout draws politicians and media types from his former digs at Washington Square Bar & Grill. Along with local luminaries, Tom Brokaw, Walter Cronkite, Tom Wolfe, and Dianne Feinstein head for Moose's when they're in town. A Mediterranean-inspired menu includes innovative appetizers, pastas, seafood, and grills. The surroundings are classic and comfortable, with views of Washington Square and Russian Hill from a front café area; counter seats have a view of the open kitchen. There's live music at night and a fine Sunday brunch. ⊠ *1652 Stockton St.,* ☎ *415/989–7800. Reservations essential. AE, DC, MC, V.*

South of Market

$$ ✕ **LuLu.** Since 1993, a seat at this boisterous restaurant has
★ been one of the hottest tickets in town. Under the high barrel-vaulted ceiling, beside a large open kitchen, diners feast on sizzling mussels roasted in an iron skillet, plus pizzas, pastas, and wood-roasted poultry, meats, and shellfish; sharing dishes is the custom here. A smaller, quieter room off to one side makes conversation easier. The café on the opposite side serves food from morning until late at night. ⊠ *816 Folsom St.,* ☎ *415/495–5775. Reservations essential. AE, DC, MC, V.*

Mexican/Latin American/Spanish

In spite of San Francisco's Mexican heritage, until recently most south-of-the-border eateries were locked into the Cal-Mex taco-enchilada-beans syndrome. Now several restaurants offer a broader spectrum of Mexican and Latin American cooking, as well as Caribbean and Spanish food.

Cow Hollow/Marina

$$ ✕ **Café Marimba.** Fanciful folk art adorns the walls of this colorful Mexican café, where an open kitchen turns out contemporary renditions of regional specialties: Silken mole *negro* (sauce of chilies and chocolate) from Oaxaca; shrimp prepared with roasted onions and tomatoes Zihuatanejo-style; and chicken with a marinade from the Yucatán stuffed into an excellent taco. Although the food is treated to many innovative touches, authenticity plays a strong role. ⊠ *2317 Chestnut St.,* ☎ *415/776–1506. MC, V. No lunch Mon.*

Russian Hill

$$ ✕ **Zarzuela.** The small, crowded but charming storefront serves nearly 40 different hot and cold tapas plus some dozen main courses. There is a tapa to suit every palate, from poached octopus atop new potatoes and hot garlic-flecked shrimp to slabs of Manchego cheese with paper-thin slices of serrano ham. The paella of saffron-scented rice weighed down with prawns, mussels, and clams is guaranteed to make even the most unsentimental Madrileño homesick. ⊠ *2000 Hyde St.,* ☎ *415/346–0800. MC, V. Reservations not accepted. Closed Sun.*

South of Market

$$ ✕ **Thirstybear.** Near the San Francisco Museum of Modern Art, Thirstybear is a combination brew pub and tapas outpost. The cavernous interior, rustic brick walls, and shiny tanks holding 7,000 homemade brews is cool and utilitarian, but the small plates of garlic-and-sherry-infused fish cheeks, steamed mussels, grilled garlic-studded shrimp, and white beans with sausage and aioli will warm you right up. Bigger appetites can dig into paella Valenciana. ⊠ *661 Howard St.,* ☎ *415/974–0905. MC, V. No lunch weekends.*

Old San Francisco

Some landmark restaurants don't fit neatly into any ethnic category. You might call them Continental or French or even American. But dating to the turn of the century or earlier—or appearing to do so—they exude the traditions and aura of Old San Francisco. The oldest of all, Tadich Grill, is really a seafood restaurant (☞ Seafood, *below*).

Financial District

$$$ ✕ **Garden Court.** The Palace Hotel is the setting of this quintessential Old San Francisco restaurant. From breakfast until the early dinner hours, light splashes through the beautiful stained-glass ceiling and against the towering Ionic columns and crystal chandeliers. The menu includes some famous dishes devised by Palace chefs early in this century—Green Goddess salad, for example—and the extravagant Sunday buffet brunch takes center stage as one of the city's great traditions. ⊠ *Market and New Montgomery Sts.,* ☎ *415/546–5011. Reservations essential. Jacket required. AE, DC, MC, V.*

Seafood

Like all port cities, San Francisco takes pride in its seafood, even though less than half the fish served here is from local waters. In winter and spring look for fresh Dungeness crab, best served just-cooked and cracked. In summer feast on Pacific salmon, even though imported varieties are available year-round. An abundant selection of unusual oysters is available from West Coast beds. And remember to order fresh seafood in the city's acclaimed Chinese restaurants.

Civic Center

$$ ✕ **Hayes Street Grill.** Up to 15 different kinds of seafood are chalked on the blackboard each night at this extremely popular restaurant. The fish is simply grilled, with a choice of sauces ranging from tomato salsa to a spicy Szechuan peanut concoction to beurre blanc. Appetizers are unusual, and desserts are lavish. ⊠ *320 Hayes St.,* ☎ *415/863–5545. Reservations essential. AE, D, DC, MC, V. No lunch weekends.*

Financial District

$$$ ✕ **Aqua.** This quietly elegant and ultrafashionable spot is
★   possibly the city's most important seafood restaurant ever. Chef-owner Michael Mina has a talent for creating contemporary versions of French, Italian, and American classics: mussel, crab, or lobster soufflé; chunks of lobster alongside lobster-stuffed ravioli; and ultrarare *ahi* tuna paired with foie gras are especially good. Desserts are miniature museum pieces—try the warm chocolate tart—

and the wine list is superb. ⊠ *252 California St.,* ☎ *415/956–9662. Reservations essential. AE, DC, MC, V. Closed Sun. No lunch Sat.*

$$ ✕ **Tadich Grill.** Owners and locations have changed many times since this old-timer opened during the gold rush era, but the 19th-century atmosphere remains, as does the kitchen's special way with seafood. Simple sautés are the best choices, or cioppino during crab season, and an old-fashioned house-made tartar sauce accompanies deep-fried items. There is seating at the counter as well as in private booths, but expect long lines at lunchtime. ⊠ *240 California St.,* ☎ *415/391–2373. Reservations not accepted. MC, V. Closed Sun.*

Northern Waterfront

$$ ✕ **McCormick & Kuleto's.** This seafood emporium in Ghirardelli Square is a visitor's dream come true: a fabulous view of the bay from every seat in the house; an Old San Francisco atmosphere; and dozens of fish and shellfish prepared in scores of globe-circling ways, from tacos, pot stickers, and fish cakes to grills, pastas, and stew. The food has its ups and downs—stick with the simplest preparations—but even on foggy days you can count on the view. Validated parking is available in the Ghirardelli Square garage. ⊠ *Ghirardelli Sq. at Beach and Larkin Sts.,* ☎ *415/929–1730. AE, D, DC, MC, V.*

Southeast Asian

In recent years San Franciscans have seen tremendous growth in the number of restaurants specializing in the foods of Thailand, Vietnam, Cambodia, and Singapore. The cuisines of these countries share many features but one in particular: a bouquet of herbs and spices flavors nearly every dish.

The Haight

$–$$ ✕ **Thep Phanom.** The fine Thai food and the lovely interior at this lower Haight institution keep local food critics and restaurant goers singing its praises. Duck is deliciously prepared in a variety of ways—in a fragrant curry, minced for salad, or resting atop a bed of spinach. Other specialties are seafood, stuffed chicken wings, and fried quail. A number of daily specials supplement the regular menu, and a wonderful mango sorbet is sometimes offered for dessert. ⊠ *400 Waller St.,* ☎ *415/431–2526. AE, MC, V.*

The Mission District

$–$$ ✕ **Slanted Door.** Behind the canted facade of this trendy new north Mission restaurant, you'll find what owner Charles Phan describes as "real Vietnamese home cooking." There are fresh spring rolls packed with rice noodles, pork, shrimp, and pungent mint leaves, and fried vegetarian imperial rolls concealing bean thread noodles, cabbage, and taro. Catfish arrives in a clay pot, and fried game hen is nicely sparked by a tamarind dipping sauce. The menu changes every two weeks, but popular dishes are never abandoned. ⊠ *584 Valencia St.,* ☎ *415/861–8032. MC, V. Closed Sun.*

Richmond District

$–$$ ✕ **Straits Cafe.** This highly popular restaurant serves the unique fare of Singapore, a cuisine that combines the culinary traditions of China, India, and the Malay archipelago. That exotic mix translates into complex curries, rice cooked in coconut milk, sticks of fragrant satay, and seafood noodle soups. The handsome dining room includes one wall that re-creates the old shop-house fronts of Singapore. ⊠ *3300 Geary Blvd.,* ☎ *415/668–1783. AE, MC, V.*

South of Market

$ ✕ **Manora.** Exotic, carefully prepared Thai fare is not far from Symphony Hall. The fried soft-shell crabs with a tamarind dipping sauce and the whitefish steamed in banana leaves are recommended, as are the traditional Thai curries featuring meats, poultry, or seafood. Plenty of SoMa night owls migrate here for sustenance before hitting the club scene. ⊠ *1600 Folsom St.,* ☎ *415/861–6224. MC, V. No lunch weekends.*

Steak Houses

Although San Francisco traditionally has not been a meat-and-potatoes town, it has several excellent steak houses. You can also get a good piece of beef at most of the better French, Italian, and American restaurants.

Marina

$$ ✕ **Izzy's Steak & Chop House.** Izzy Gomez was a legendary
San Francisco saloon keeper, and his namesake eatery car-
ries on the tradition. Here you'll find terrific steaks, chops,
and seafood plus all the trimmings, from cheesy scalloped
potatoes to creamed spinach. A collection of Izzy memo-
rabilia and antique advertising art covers almost every inch
of wall space. There's validated parking at the Lombard
garage. ✉ *3345 Steiner St.,* ☎ *415/563–0487. AE, DC,
MC, V. No lunch.*

Midtown

$$$ ✕ **Harris'.** Ann Harris knows her beef. She grew up on a
★   Texas cattle ranch and was married to the late Jack Har-
ris of Harris Ranch fame. In her own large, New York–style
restaurant she serves some of the best dry-aged steaks in
town, but don't overlook the starter of smoked salmon or
entrées of grilled salmon or calves' liver with onions and
bacon. There is also an extensive bar menu and a first-rate
pecan pie. ✉ *2100 Van Ness Ave.,* ☎ *415/673–1888. AE,
DC, MC, V. No lunch.*

Vegetarian

Vegetarians should also consider Indian and Southeast
Asian restaurants, as most generally offer a variety of meat-
less dishes.

Marina

$$ ✕ **Greens.** This beautiful restaurant with expansive bay
★   views is owned and operated by the Zen Buddhist Center
of Marin County. The dining room offers a wide, eclectic,
and creative spectrum of meatless cooking, and the on-site
bakery promises nirvana. Dinners are à la carte on week-
nights, but only a five-course prix fixe dinner is served on
Saturday. Sunday brunch is a good time to watch local sail-
boat owners take out their crafts. There's public parking
at Fort Mason Center. ✉ *Bldg. A, Fort Mason (enter the
fort across Marina Blvd. from Safeway),* ☎ *415/771–
6222. MC, V. No lunch Mon., no dinner Sun.*

4 Lodging

Updated
by Sharron
Wood

FEW CITIES IN THE UNITED STATES can rival
San Francisco's variety in lodging. There
are plush hotels ranked among the finest
in the world, renovated older buildings with a European
flair, and the popular chain hotels found in most cities in
the United States. One of the brightest spots in the lodging
picture is the proliferation of small bed-and-breakfasts
housed in elegant Victorian buildings, where evening hors
d'oeuvres and wine service are common practice. Another
is the growing number of modern hotels, such as the Radisson
Miyako and the Mandarin Oriental, which specialize
in attentive Asian-style hospitality.

The **San Francisco Convention and Visitors Bureau** (☎
415/391–2000) publishes a free lodging guide with a map
and a listing of all hotels. Because San Francisco is one of
the top destinations in the United States for tourists as well
as business travelers and convention goers, reservations are
always advised, especially during the May through October
peak season.

San Francisco's geography makes it conveniently compact.
No matter what their location, the hotels listed below are
on or close to public transportation lines. A few properties
on Lombard Street and in the Civic Center area have
free parking, but hotels in the Union Square and Nob Hill
areas almost invariably charge $17–$26 a day for a spot
in their garage.

Although not as high as the rates in New York, San Francisco
hotel prices are steep. Rates for double rooms downtown
and at the wharf start at about $120. Adding to the
expense is the city's 14% transient occupancy tax. The good
news is that because of the hotel building boom of the late
1980s, there is now an oversupply of rooms, which has led
to frequent discounts. Check for special rates and packages
when making reservations. For those in search of true budget
accommodations (under $50), try the Adelaide Inn (☞
Union Square/Downtown, *below*) or the YMCA Central
Branch (✉ 220 Golden Gate Ave., ☎ 415/885–0460).

An alternative to hotels and motels is staying in private homes
and apartments, available through **American Family Inn/Bed**

& Breakfast San Francisco (✉ Box 420009, 94142, ☎ 415/931–3083, 𝔽𝔸𝕏 415/921–2273), **Bed & Breakfast California** (✉ 205 Park Rd., Suite 209, Burlingame 94010, ☎ 650/696–1690 or 800/872–4500, 𝔽𝔸𝕏 650/696–1699), and **American Property Exchange** (✉ 2800 Lombard St., San Francisco 94109, ☎ 415/863–8484 or 800/747–7784, 𝔽𝔸𝕏 415/440–1008).

The lodgings we list are the best in each price range:

CATEGORY	COST*
$$$$	over $175
$$$	$120–$175
$$	$80–$120
$	under $80

All prices are for a standard double room, excluding 14% tax.

Union Square/Downtown

The largest variety and greatest concentration of hotels is in the city's downtown hub, Union Square, where you'll find the best shopping, the theater district, and convenient transportation to every part of San Francisco.

$$$$ 🏨 **Campton Place.** Behind a simple brownstone facade
★ with a white awning, quiet reigns. Highly attentive personal service—from unpacking assistance to nightly turndown—begins the moment uniformed doormen greet you outside the marble-floor lobby. Rooms, though small and not as flashy as those at some other luxury hotels, are supremely elegant with Asian touches in subtle earth tones. They overlook an atrium, which lends a cozy, residential feel. The Campton Place Restaurant, listed as one of San Francisco's best by *Gourmet* magazine in 1996, is famed for its breakfast. Wednesday martini nights (5:30–8:30) in the lounge, with specially priced martinis and live music, have become a favorite midweek cruising ground for the downtown crowd. ✉ *340 Stockton St., 94108, ☎ 415/781–5555 or 800/235–4300, 𝔽𝔸𝕏 415/955–5536. 117 rooms. Restaurant, bar, in-room safes, minibars, no-smoking rooms, room service, laundry service and dry cleaning, concierge, meeting rooms, parking (fee). AE, DC, MC, V.*

Downtown San Francisco Lodging

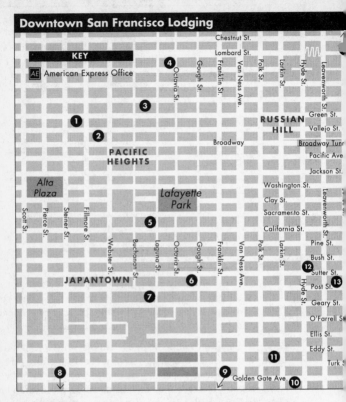

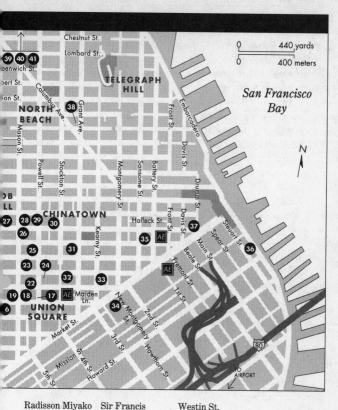

Chestnut St.

Lombard St.

TELEGRAPH HILL

NORTH BEACH

Greenwich St.

bert St.

ion St.

Mason St.

Powell St.

Stockton St.

Columbus Ave.

Grant Ave.

San Francisco Bay

Embarcadero

Front St.

Davis St.

Battery St.

Sansome St.

Montgomery St.

Kearny St.

CHINATOWN

Halleck St.

Davis St.

Front St.

Drumm St.

Spear St.

Steuart St.

Main St.

Beale St.

Fremont St.

1st St.

2nd St.

New Montgomery St.

Hawthorn St.

3rd St.

Mission St.

4th St.

5th St.

Howard St.

Market St.

UNION SQUARE

Maiden Ln.

80

TO AIRPORT

0   440 yards
0   400 meters

N

Radisson Miyako Hotel, **7**

Renaissance Stanford Court, **29**

Ritz-Carlton, San Francisco, **30**

San Remo, **39**

Sherman House, **2**

Sir Francis Drake, **24**

Travelodge Hotel at Fisherman's Wharf, **41**

Tuscan Inn, **40**

Union Street Inn, **1**

Vintage Court, **25**

Westin St. Francis, **17**

York Hotel, **12**

$$$$ 🖭 **The Clift.** This Grand Heritage hotel towers over the theater district; its crisp, forest green awnings and formal door service provide subtle hints of the elegance within. In the lobby, dark paneling and enormous chandeliers speak of grandeur. Rooms, some with dark woods and burgundies, others refreshingly pastel, all have large writing desks, plants, and flowers. The Clift is noted for its swift personalized service; a phone call will get you anything from complimentary limousine service to a chocolate cake. Sample a cocktail in the dramatic art deco Redwood Room lounge, complete with chandeliers and a sweeping redwood bar. ⊠ *495 Geary St., 94102,* ☎ *415/775–4700 or 800/652–5438,* 📠 *415/441–4621. 329 rooms. Restaurant, bar, in-room modem lines, minibars, no-smoking floor, room service, exercise room, laundry service and dry cleaning, concierge, meeting rooms, parking (fee). AE, DC, MC, V.*

$$$$ 🖭 **Prescott Hotel.** Gourmets savor this plush hotel's part-
★ nership with Wolfgang Puck's Postrio (☞ American *in* Chapter 3), one of San Francisco's best restaurants. Guests can order room service from the restaurant or dine at tables reserved for hotel guests—no small perk considering it can otherwise take months to get in. The Prescott's rooms, which vary only in size and shape, are traditional in style and decorated in a rich hunter green; bathrooms have marble-top sinks and gold fixtures. There's a fireplace in the hunting lodge–style living room—a perfect setting for the complimentary coffee and tea services and evening wine and cheese receptions. ⊠ *545 Post St., 94102,* ☎ *415/563–0303 or 800/283–7322,* 📠 *415/563–6831. 165 rooms. Restaurant, bar, lobby lounge, in-room modem lines, no-smoking floors, room service, concierge, business services, meeting rooms, parking (fee). AE, D, DC, MC, V.*

$$$$ 🖭 **Westin St. Francis.** Guests as illustrious as Emperor Hirohito, Queen Elizabeth II, and presidents have stayed here since it opened in 1904. No wonder; with an imposing facade, black marble lobby, and gold-top columns, the St. Francis looks more like a great public building than a hotel. The Compass Rose bar and restaurant is a retreat from the bustle of Union Square, especially for those in a romantic frame of mind. Many rooms in the original building are small, but all retain their original Victorian-style moldings and have Empire-style furnishings. Rooms in the modern tower are larger, with Oriental-style lacquered furniture; ask for a room above the 15th floor for a spectacular view of the city. ⊠ *335 Powell St., 94102,* ☎ *415/397–7000 or 800/228–3000,* ℻ *415/774–0124. 1,192 rooms. 3 restaurants, 2 bars, in-room modem lines, in-room safes, no-smoking floors, room service, exercise room, nightclub, concierge, business services, meeting rooms, travel services, parking (fee).* AE, D, DC, MC, V.

$$$ 🏨 **Galleria Park.** A few blocks east of Union Square, this
★ hotel with a black marble facade is close to the Chinatown Gate and the Crocker Galleria, one of San Francisco's most elegant shopping areas. The staff is remarkably pleasant and helpful. The comfortable rooms all have floral bedspreads, stylish striped wallpaper, and white furniture that includes a writing desk. You can sip complimentary coffee and tea in the mornings and wine in the evenings by the lobby's fireplace. Adjoining the hotel is Perry's Downtown (*see* American *in* Chapter 3), a casual steak-and-burger eatery. ⊠ *191 Sutter St., 94104,* ☎ *415/781–3060 or 800/792–9639,* ℻ *415/433–4409. 177 rooms. 2 restaurants, in-room modem lines, minibars, no-smoking floors, room service, exercise room, jogging, concierge, business services, meeting rooms.* AE, D, DC, MC, V.

$$$ 🏨 **Hotel Diva.** A gray awning and burnished silver facade give this reasonably priced hotel a slick, high-tech look that sets it apart from others. The futuristic decor extends to the rooms, which have angular sofas, wire-frame chairs, and black-lacquered furniture. Although the Diva's proximity to the Curran Theater attracts actors, musicians, and others of an artistic bent, it's also popular with business travelers, who have free access to the tiny business center, and families. ⊠ *440 Geary St., 94102,* ☎ *415/885–0200 or 800/553–1900,* ℻ *415/346–6613. 110 rooms. Restaurant, in-room modem lines, in-room safes, no-smoking floor, exercise room, business services, meeting room.* AE, D, DC, MC, V.

$$$ 🏨 **Hotel Monaco.** Unquestionably the hottest hotel in town,
★ the Hotel Monaco, with its yellow beaux arts facade, stands in stark contrast to its more stately neighbor, the Clift. The contrast continues inside, where a French inglenook fireplace climbs almost two stories above the lobby toward the

three huge domes of a hand-painted vaulted ceiling. Though small, the rooms are comfortable and inviting, with Chinese-inspired armoires, high-back upholstered chairs, and in the outer rooms, bay window seats overlooking the theater district. The riot of stripes and colors may strike some guests as a bit outré, but it's been done so tastefully you can't help but appreciate the flair. ⊠ *501 Geary St., 94102,* ☎ *415/292–0100 or 800/214–4220,* 𝔽𝔸𝕏 *415/292–0111. 201 rooms. Restaurant, bar, in-room modem lines, no-smoking rooms, room service, spa, laundry service and dry cleaning, business services, parking (fee). AE, D, DC, MC, V.*

$$$ 🏨 **Hotel Rex.** Literary and artistic creativity are celebrated in style here, where thousands of books, largely antiquarian, line the clubby, 1920s-style lobby. Original artwork adorns the walls, and the proprietors even host book readings and roundtable discussions in the common areas. Upstairs, quotations from works by California writers are painted on the terra-cotta-color walls near the elevator landings. Rooms have writing desks and lamps with whimsically hand-painted shades. Striped bedspreads and carpets and restored period furnishings continue to evoke the spirit of 1920s salon society. ⊠ *562 Sutter St., 94102,* ☎ *415/433–4434,* 𝔽𝔸𝕏 *415/433–3695. 94 rooms. Bar, lobby lounge, in-room modem lines, minibars, no-smoking rooms, laundry service and dry cleaning, concierge, parking (fee). AE, D, DC, MC, V.*

$$$ 🏨 **Hotel Triton.** The Triton just may be the zaniest hostelry in town. Guests enter via a whimsical lobby of three-legged furniture, star-patterned carpeting, and inverted gilt pillars—stylized spoofs of upside-down Roman columns. The hotel caters to fashion, entertainment, music, and film-industry types, who seem to appreciate the iridescent pink-and-gold-painted rooms with S-curve dervish chairs, curly-neck lamps, and oddball light fixtures. On the downside, rooms are uncommonly small; if you care about space, try a junior suite. The trendy newsstand–coffeehouse–dining room Café de la Presse is attached to the hotel. ⊠ *342 Grant Ave., 94108,* ☎ *415/394–0500 or 800/433–6611,* 𝔽𝔸𝕏 *415/394–0555. 140 rooms. In-room modem lines, no-smoking floors, exercise room, laundry service, business services, meeting rooms, parking (fee). AE, D, MC, V.*

$$$ ⚿ **Inn at Union Square.** With its tiny but captivating lobby with trompe l'oeil bookshelves painted on the walls, this inn feels like someone's home. Comfortable Georgian-style rooms with sumptuous goose-down pillows promote indolence; brass lion's-head door knockers are a unique touch. Guests lounge in front of the fireplaces in each floor's tiny sitting area, and with good reason: By the time the staff clears away the afternoon tea and pastries, they're already setting out the complimentary evening wine and hors d'oeuvres. Continental breakfast is also complimentary and is served in the sitting area or in your room. Tips are not accepted. ✉ *440 Post St., 94102,* ☎ *415/397–3510 or 800/288–4346,* ℻ *415/989–0529. 30 rooms. No-smoking floor, parking (fee). AE, DC, MC, V.*

$$$ ⚿ **Sir Francis Drake.** Beefeater-costumed doormen (including the internationally renowned Tom Sweeney) welcome you into the regal lobby, which has wrought-iron balustrades, chandeliers, and Italian marble. The guest rooms have a simpler decor with California-style furnishings and floral-print fabrics. On the top floor, Harry Denton's Starlight Room has been all the rage since its opening in September 1995. The hotel's surprisingly affordable restaurant, Scala's Bistro (☞ Italian *in* Chapter 3), serves excellent food in its dramatic though somewhat noisy dining room. ✉ *450 Powell St., 94102,* ☎ *415/392–7755 or 800/227–5480,* ℻ *415/395–8599. 417 rooms. 2 restaurants, in-room modem lines, no-smoking rooms, nightclub, concierge, meeting rooms, parking (fee). AE, D, DC, MC, V.*

$$$ ⚿ **Vintage Court.** This bit of the Napa Valley just off Union Square has inviting rooms—some with sunny window seats—with jade and rose floral fabrics. Complimentary wine served every evening in front of the lobby fireplace and a deluxe Continental breakfast have created a congenial atmosphere without driving prices up. Just off the lobby is Masa's (☞ French *in* Chapter 3), one of the city's most celebrated French restaurants. Guests have access to an affiliated health club one block away. ✉ *650 Bush St., 94108,* ☎ *415/392–4666 or 800/654–1100,* ℻ *415/433–4065. 107 rooms. Restaurant, bar, minibars, no-smoking floor, refrigerators, parking (fee). AE, D, DC, MC, V.*

$$$ 🏨 **York Hotel.** Hitchcock fans may recognize the exterior of this reasonably priced, family-owned hotel; it's the building where Kim Novak as Judy Barton stayed in *Vertigo*. Inside, the ornate, high-ceiling lobby gives the hotel a touch of elegance. The moderate-size rooms are a tasteful mix of Mediterranean styles; all have huge closets. The Plush Room cabaret, where well-known entertainers perform four to five times a week, is the York's drawing card. This is perhaps the most gay-friendly of San Francisco's more elegant hotels. Complimentary Continental breakfast is included. ✉ *940 Sutter St., 94109,* ☎ *415/885-6800 or 800/808-9675,* 🖷 *415/885-2115. 96 rooms. Bar, no-smoking floor, exercise room, nightclub, concierge, parking (fee). AE, D, DC, MC, V.*

$$ 🏨 **The Andrews.** This Queen Anne–style abode with a dark-gray-and-white facade began its life as the Sultan Turkish Baths in 1905. Today Victorian antique reproductions, old-fashioned flower curtains with lace sheers, iron bedsteads, and good-size closets more than make up for the diminutive size of guest rooms (the scrupulously clean bathrooms are even smaller). A buffet-style Continental breakfast is served daily on every floor. Fino, the hotel restaurant, has been praised for its pizza and its carbonara, and guests enjoy complimentary wine nightly. ✉ *624 Post St., 94109,* ☎ *415/563-6877 or 800/926-3739,* 🖷 *415/ 928-6919. 48 rooms. Restaurant, no-smoking rooms, concierge, parking (fee). AE, MC, V.*

$$ 🏨 **Commodore International.** Entering the lobby is like stepping onto the main deck of an ocean liner of yore: Neodeco chairs look like the backdrop for a film about transatlantic crossings; and steps away is the Titanic Cafe, where goldfish bowls and bathysphere-inspired lights add to the sea-cruise mood. The fairly large rooms with monster closets are painted in soft yellows and golds and decorated with framed photographs of San Francisco landmarks. The hotel's Red Room is a startlingly scarlet boîte. ✉ *825 Sutter St., 94109,* ☎ *415/923-6800 or 800/338-6848,* 🖷 *415/923-6804. 113 rooms. Restaurant, no-smoking rooms, nightclub, laundry service and dry cleaning, parking (fee). AE, D, MC, V.*

$$ 🏨 **The Maxwell.** Formerly known as The Raphael, The Maxwell is a simple but stylish hotel just a few blocks from Union Square. Behind the dramatic black and red curtains, the Victorian-style lobby welcomes you with a green velvet sofa and boldly patterned chairs. Rooms have a clubby, retro feel and are decorated in deep jewel tones. The cocktail-lounge ambience at the new Gracie's Restaurant provides a stylish setting for a menu of "re-invented classics" and weekend live jazz music. ✉ 386 Geary St., 94102, ☎ 415/986–2000 or 888/734–6299, ℻ 415/397–2447. 153 rooms. Restaurant, bar, in-room modem lines, no-smoking floor, room service, laundry service, concierge, parking (fee). AE, D, DC, MC, V.

$ ⊞ **Adelaide Inn.** The bedspreads at this quiet retreat may not match the drapes or carpets, and the floors may creak, but the rooms are sunny, clean, and cheap: $42 to $48 for a double, each with shared bath. Tucked away in an alley, the funky European-style pension hosts many guests from Germany, France, and Italy. ✉ 5 Isadora Duncan Ct., at Taylor between Geary and Post Sts., 94102, ☎ 415/441–2474 or 415/441–2261, ℻ 415/441–0161. 18 rooms. Breakfast room, refrigerators. AE, MC, V.

Financial District

High-rise growth in San Francisco's Financial District has turned it into a mini-Manhattan and a spectacular sight by night. Shoppers and sightseers enjoy easy access to nearby Union Square, the Embarcadero, Pier 39 at Fisherman's Wharf, Market Street shops, and the South of Market area's late-night hot spots. Many restaurants and bars in the neighborhood itself close soon after the last commuters catch their BART train home.

$$$$ ⊞ **Hyatt Regency.** The gray-concrete bunkerlike exterior of the Hyatt Regency, at the foot of Market Street, is an unlikely introduction to the spectacular 17-story atrium lobby within. The Embarcadero Center, with more than 100 shops and restaurants, is its neighbor; and the Equinox, San Francisco's only revolving rooftop restaurant, sits atop the hotel like a crown jewel. Rooms, some with bay-view balconies, are decorated in two styles: Both have cherry-wood furniture, but one strikes a more masculine tone with a black-and-brown color scheme, while the other has soft rose-and-

plum combinations. ⊠ *5 Embarcadero Center, 94111,* ☎ *415/788–1234 or 800/233–1234,* FAX *415/398–2567. 805 rooms. 2 restaurants, bar, lobby lounge, no-smoking floor, room service, exercise room, concierge, concierge floor, parking (fee). AE, D, DC, MC, V.*

$$$$ ☎ **Mandarin Oriental.** Since the Mandarin comprises the
★   top 11 floors (38 to 48) of San Francisco's third-tallest building—the First Interstate Center—all rooms provide panoramic vistas of the city and beyond. As striking as the views are the glass-enclosed sky bridges that connect the towers of the hotel. Rooms are done in light creamy yellow with black accents; those in the front tower fill up quickly because of their dramatic ocean views. The Mandarin Rooms in each tower have bathtubs flanked by windows and decadent bathing accessories. The adjoining restaurant Silks earns rave reviews for its innovative California-Asian cuisine. ⊠ *222 Sansome St., 94104,* ☎ *415/885–0999 or 800/622–0404,* FAX *415/433–0289. 158 rooms. Lobby lounge, in-room modem lines, minibars, no-smoking floor, room service, laundry service and dry cleaning, concierge, business services, meeting rooms, parking (fee). AE, D, DC, MC, V.*

$$$$ ☎ **Palace Hotel.** This landmark hotel—with a guest list that has included Enrico Caruso, Woodrow Wilson, and Amelia Earhart—was the epitome of luxury when it opened in 1875. Today its historic splendor is best seen in the stunning entryway and the belle epoque Garden Court restaurant, with its graceful chandeliers and lead-glass ceiling. After the lavish public spaces, the rooms seem uninspired, although modern conveniences, like TVs inside the mahogany armoires, are well integrated into the decor. Though service is disappointing, the hotel's location and business services make it a logical choice for business travelers. The hotel restaurant, Maxfield's, is named for the Maxfield Parrish mural *The Pied Piper* hanging over the bar. ⊠ *2 New Montgomery St., 94105,* ☎ *415/392–8600 or 800/325–3535,* FAX *415/543–0671. 550 rooms. 3 restaurants, bar, room service, indoor lap pool, health club, laundry service, business services, parking (fee). AE, D, DC, MC, V.*

$$$ ☎ **Harbor Court.** This cozy hotel, formerly a YMCA, is noted
★   for the exemplary service of its friendly staff. Some guest rooms overlook the bay; others face a courtyard with a lush

English-Italian garden. In the evening complimentary wine is served in the lounge, sometimes accompanied by live guitar. Guests have free access to YMCA facilities (including a 150-ft heated indoor pool), on one side of the hotel, and to Harry Denton's Bar and Grill, on the other. There's also a complimentary limousine service to the Financial District. ✉ *165 Steuart St., 94105,* ☎ *415/882–1300 or 800/346–0555,* 𝔽𝔸𝕏 *415/882–1313. 131 rooms. In-room modem lines, minibars, no-smoking floor, room service, business services, parking (fee). AE, D, DC, MC, V.*

Nob Hill

Synonymous with San Francisco's high society, Nob Hill contains some of the city's best-known luxury hotels. Most have spectacular city and bay views and all have noted gourmet restaurants. Cable car lines that cross Nob Hill make the short but steep trek from Union Square easier.

$$$$ ⊞ **The Fairmont.** Perched atop Nob Hill and queen of all ★ she surveys, the Fairmont, which served as the model for the St. Gregory in the TV series *Hotel,* has the most awe-inspiring lobby in the city, with a soaring vaulted ceiling; towering, hand-painted faux-marble columns; gilt mirrors; red-velvet upholstered chairs; and a grand wraparound staircase. The tower rooms, which have spectacular city and bay views, reflect a more modern style than their smaller Victorian counterparts in the older building. The South Pacific–theme Tonga Room hosts San Francisco's busiest happy hour, and the New Orleans Room spotlights famous talents such as James Brown and local luminaries such as Pete Escovedo. ✉ *950 Mason St., 94108,* ☎ *415/772–5000 or 800/527–4727,* 𝔽𝔸𝕏 *415/837–0587. 596 rooms. 4 restaurants, 5 bars, room service, barber shop, beauty salon, spa, health club, laundry service and dry cleaning, concierge, business services, car rental. AE, D, DC, MC, V.*

$$$$ ⊞ **The Huntington.** Across from Grace Cathedral, the red-brick Huntington provides a quiet alternative to the larger, more famous hotels down the street. The staff is known for attentive personal service: You might be greeted by name as you return from your evening out; but the privacy of the hotel's celebrated guests is impeccably preserved. Rooms and suites reflect the Huntington's traditional style, albeit with a '90s bent. Opulent materials such as raw silks and velvets are mixed and matched in a rich color scheme of cocoa, gold, and burgundy, with florals and stripes. Guests can use the health club at the nearby Fairmont for a $15 per day fee. ✉ *1075 California St., 94108,* ☎ *415/474–5400 or 800/227–4683; 800/652–1539 in CA;* ℻ *415/474–6227. 140 rooms. Restaurant, bar, in-room modem lines, no-smoking rooms, room service, laundry service and dry cleaning, concierge, meeting rooms. AE, D, DC, MC, V.*

$$$$ 🏨 **Mark Hopkins Inter-Continental.** The circular drive to this Nob Hill landmark across from the Fairmont leads to a lobby with floor-to-ceiling mirrors and marble floors. The rooms, with dramatic neoclassic furnishings of gray, silver, and khaki and bold leaf-print bedspreads, lead into bathrooms lined with Italian marble. Rooms on high floors have views of either the Golden Gate Bridge or the downtown cityscape. No visit would be complete without a gander at the panoramic views from the newly renovated Top of the Mark, *the* rooftop lounge in San Francisco since 1939 (open evenings only). ✉ *999 California St., 94108,* ☎ *415/392–3434 or 800/327–0200,* ℻ *415/421–3302. 392 rooms. 2 restaurants, 2 lounges, room service, exercise room, laundry service and dry cleaning, concierge, business services, car rental. AE, D, DC, MC, V.*

$$$$ 🏨 **Renaissance Stanford Court.** Despite its relatively large size, the Stanford Court has a distinctly residential feel. The lobby is dominated by a stained-glass dome, a dramatic mural of early San Francisco scenes, and high-quality arts and antiques—look for the Maxfield Parrish painting *Old White Birch*. Rooms invariably achieve understated elegance with a mix of English country manor–style furnishings accented with Asian artwork and accessories. The hotel's restaurant, Fournou's Ovens—famed for its 54-square-ft roasting oven, Mediterranean-influenced cuisine, and world-class wine cellar—is usually packed. ✉ *905 California St., 94108,* ☎ *415/989–3500 or 800/227–4736; 800/622–0957 in CA;* ℻ *415/391–0513. 402 rooms. Restaurant, bar, in-room modem lines, no-smoking floor, exercise room, piano, concierge, business services, meeting rooms, parking (fee). AE, DC, MC, V.*

Pick up the phone.

Pick up the miles.

Now when you sign up with MCI you can receive up to 8,000 bonus frequent flyer miles on one of seven major airlines.

Then earn another 5 miles for every dollar you spend on a variety of MCI services, including MCI Card® calls from virtually anywhere in the world.*

You're going to use these services anyway. Why not rack up the miles while you're doing it?

Is this a great time, or what? :-)

Urban planning.

CITYPACKS

The ultimate guide to the city—a complete pocket guide plus a full-size color map.

$$$$ ⊞ **Ritz-Carlton, San Francisco.** Consistently rated one of the
★ top hotels in the world, the Ritz-Carlton is a stunning tribute to beauty, splendor, and warm, sincere service. Beyond
the neoclassic facade, crystal chandeliers illuminate an opulent lobby adorned with Georgian antiques and museum-
quality 18th- and 19th-century paintings. The elegant and
spacious guest rooms reflect this grandeur, as do the lavish Italian marble baths. The hotel has a newly renovated
fitness center with an indoor swimming pool, saunas, a
whirlpool, and in-room massages. The renowned Dining
Room enjoys a newly invigorated following, thanks to celebrated chef Sylvain Portay, originally from New York's Le
Cirque. Afternoon tea in the Lobby Lounge—which overlooks the hotel's beautifully landscaped garden courtyard—
is a San Francisco institution (*see* Piano Bars *in* Chapter 5).
⊠ *600 Stockton St., at California St., 94108,* ☎ *415/296–
7465 or 800/241–3333,* 䕺 *415/296–8261. 336 rooms. 2
restaurants, bar, lobby lounge, laundry service and dry
cleaning, concierge, business services, meeting rooms, parking (fee). AE, D, DC, MC, V.*

Fisherman's Wharf/North Beach

Fisherman's Wharf, San Francisco's top tourist attraction,
is also the most popular area for lodging. All accommodations are within blocks from restaurants, shops, and
cable car lines. Because of city ordinances, no hotel exceeds
four stories, so this is not the area for fantastic views of the
city or the bay. Reservations are essential, sometimes weeks
in advance during peak summer months, when hotel rates
rise by as much as 30%. Some street-side rooms are noisy.

$$$$ ⊞ **Hyatt at Fisherman's Wharf.** Location is the key to this
hotel's popularity: It's within walking distance of Ghirardelli Square, the Cannery, Pier 39, Aquatic Park, and docks
for ferries and bay cruises. It's also across the street from a
cable car turnaround. The moderate-size guest rooms, a med-
ley of greens and burgundies with dark woods and brass fixtures, have double-pane windows to keep out the often
considerable street noise. Each floor has a laundry room.
In the North Point Lounge, part of the hotel's conference
center, a domed Tiffany skylight crowns a large, comfy

meeting area with a fireplace and fountain. ⊠ *555 North Point St., 94133,* ☎ *415/563–1234 or 800/233–1234,* fax *415/563–2218. 313 rooms. Restaurant, sports bar, no-smoking floor, pool, outdoor hot tub, health club, coin laundry, meeting rooms, parking (fee). AE, D, DC, MC, V.*

$$$ **Tuscan Inn.** The major attraction here is the friendly, attentive staff, which provides services such as a complimentary limousine to the Financial District. The condolike exterior of the inn gives little indication of the charm of the relatively small, Italian-influenced guest rooms, with their white-pine furniture and floral fabrics. Room service is provided by Cafe Pescatore, the Italian seafood restaurant off the lobby. Morning coffee, tea, and biscotti are complimentary, and wine is served in the early evening. ⊠ *425 North Point St., at Mason St., 94133,* ☎ *415/561–1100 or 800/648–4626,* fax *415/561–1199. 220 rooms. Restaurant, room service, meeting rooms. AE, D, DC, MC, V.*

$$ **Hotel Bohème.** In the middle of historic North Beach, this little bargain gives guests a taste of the past. The small rooms, decorated with European armoires, bistro tables, and memorabilia from the '50s and '60s, recall the beat generation. Coral-color walls and handmade lampshades complete the nostalgic mood. Enjoy complimentary sherry in the lobby while you decide which of the many nearby Italian restaurants and cafés to visit. ⊠ *444 Columbus Ave., 94133,* ☎ *415/433–9111,* fax *415/362–6292. 16 rooms. AE, D, MC, V.*

$$ **Travelodge Hotel at Fisherman's Wharf.** The Travelodge is the only bay-front hotel at Fisherman's Wharf and is known for its reasonable rates. The higher-price rooms on the upper floors have balconies that provide open views of Alcatraz and overlook a landscaped courtyard and pool. Rooms are simply and brightly furnished with lacquered blond-wood furniture, leather chairs, and rose-color fabrics. Many families stay here, and 80% of the guests are international. ⊠ *250 Beach St., 94133,* ☎ *415/392–6700 or 800/578–7878,* fax *415/986–7853. 250 rooms. 3 restaurants, no-smoking rooms, pool, free parking. AE, D, DC, MC, V.*

$ ★   **San Remo.** This blue-and-white Italianate Victorian a couple of blocks from Fisherman's Wharf has a down-home, slightly tatty elegance. The somewhat cramped rooms are filled with furniture: vanities, pedestal sinks, ceiling fans, antique armoires, and brass, iron, or wooden beds. Guests share six shower rooms, one bathtub chamber, and six sparkling clean toilets with brass pull chains and oak tanks. The penthouse has a 360-degree view of the city and a private bath and is often requested by honeymooners and other romantics. ⊠ *2237 Mason St., 94133,* ☎ *415/776–8688 or 800/352–7366,* ℻ *415/776–2811. 62 rooms. No-smoking rooms, parking (fee). AE, DC, MC, V.*

Pacific Heights, Cow Hollow, and the Marina

Lombard Street, a major traffic corridor leading to the Golden Gate Bridge, borders San Francisco's poshest neighborhoods: Pacific Heights, Cow Hollow, and the Marina. The cheapest accommodations are along Lombard Street, although prices start to climb around Union Street, with its myriad shops and restaurants. The Marina area is the quietest.

$$$$ 🏨 **Sherman House.** This magnificent Italianate mansion at
★ the foot of residential Pacific Heights is San Francisco's most luxurious small hotel. Rooms are individually decorated with Biedermeier, English Jacobean, or French Second Empire antiques. The decadent mood is enhanced by tapestry-like canopies over four-poster featherbeds, wood-burning fireplaces with marble mantels, and sumptuous bathrooms, some with whirlpool baths. The six romantic suites attract honeymooners, and the elegant in-house dining room serves superb French-inspired cuisine. ⊠ *2160 Green St., 94123,* ☎ *415/563–3600 or 800/424–5777,* ℻ *415/563–1882. 14 rooms. Dining room, room service, in-room VCRs, piano, concierge, airport shuttle. AE, DC, MC, V.*

$$$ 🏨 **Union Street Inn.** This ivy-draped 1902 Edwardian home
★ is a delightful B&B filled with antiques. Equipped with candles, fresh flowers, and wine glasses, rooms are popular with honeymooners and other romantics. The very private Carriage House, which has its own whirlpool tub, is separated from the main house by an old-fashioned English garden complete with lemon trees. An elaborate complimentary breakfast is served to guests in the parlor, in the garden, or in their rooms. ⊠ *2229 Union St., 94123,* ☎ *415/346–*

0424, FAX 415/922–8046. *6 rooms. Breakfast room, no-smoking rooms, parking (fee). AE, MC, V.*

$$–$$$ ⊞ **Bed and Breakfast Inn.** Hidden in an alleyway off Union Street, between Buchanan and Laguna, this ivy-covered Victorian is San Francisco's first B&B. Pierre Deux and Laura Ashley are the inspirations of the English country–style rooms, which are full of antiques, plants, and floral paintings. Though the rooms with shared bath are quite small, the Mayfair, a private apartment above the main house, comes with a living room, kitchenette, and spiral staircase leading to a sleeping loft. The Garden Suite, a larger, more deluxe apartment, has a country kitchen, whirlpool bath, and room for four guests. ⊠ *4 Charlton Ct., at Union St., 94123,* ☎ *415/921–9784. 6 rooms, 1 with bath, 2 apartments. Breakfast room, parking (fee). No credit cards.*

$ ⊞ **Marina Inn.** This inn five blocks from the Marina offers B&B-style accommodations at motel prices. English country–style rooms are sparsely appointed, with a queen-size two-poster bed, private bath, and pine furniture; the wallpaper and bedspreads are aggressively floral. Some rooms facing Octavia and Lombard streets have bay windows. Complimentary Continental breakfast and afternoon sherry are served in the central sitting room. ⊠ *3110 Octavia St., at Lombard St., 94123,* ☎ *415/928–1000 or 800/274–1420,* FAX *415/928–5909. 40 rooms. Lobby lounge, no-smoking floor, barbershop, beauty salon. AE, MC, V.*

Civic Center/Van Ness

Small hotels here host fans of the symphony and opera, which perform nearby, and those looking for a slightly better deal than they'll find in the ritzier Union Square area. The neighborhood is experiencing a renaissance of sorts: Fine restaurants flank Van Ness Avenue, and smaller, hipper places are west of Van Ness on Hayes Street.

$$$ ⊞ **The Archbishops Mansion.** Everything is extravagantly
★   romantic here, starting with the cavernous common areas, where a chandelier hangs above a 1904 Bechstein grand piano owned by Noel Coward. The 15 guest rooms, each named for a famous opera, are decorated with intricately carved antiques; many have Jacuzzi tubs or fireplaces.

Though not within walking distance of many restaurants or attractions, its perch on Alamo Square near the Painted Ladies Victorian homes makes for a scenic, relaxed setting. Enjoy a complimentary Continental breakfast in the ornate dining room or in your own suite; there's also an afternoon wine service. ⊠ *1000 Fulton St., 94117,* ☎ *415/563−7872 or 800/543−5820,* 𝔽𝔸𝕏 *415/885−3193. 15 rooms. Breakfast room, lobby lounge, no-smoking rooms, in-room VCRs, piano, meeting room, free parking. AE, MC, V.*

$$$ ⊡ **Hotel Majestic.** One of San Francisco's original grand ho-
★ tels, this five-story yellow-and-white 1902 Edwardian surrounds you with elegance. Most of the romantic guest rooms have gas fireplaces, a mix of French and English antiques, and either a large, hand-painted, four-poster canopied bed or two-poster bonnet twin beds. Afternoons bring complimentary sherry and homemade biscotti in the exquisite lobby, replete with black-marble stairs, antique chandeliers, plush Victorian chairs, and a white-marble fireplace. The hotel's renowned Café Majestic has an innovative menu of California cuisine with an Asian touch. ⊠ *1500 Sutter St., 94109,* ☎ *415/441−1100 or 800/869−8966,* 𝔽𝔸𝕏 *415/673−7331. 57 rooms. Restaurant, bar, laundry service and dry cleaning, parking (fee). AE, DC, MC, V.*

$$$ ⊡ **Inn at the Opera.** This seven-story hotel a block or so
★ from city hall, Davies Hall, and the War Memorial Opera House hosts the likes of Pavarotti and Baryshnikov, as well as lesser lights of the music, dance, and opera worlds. Behind the recently renovated marble-floor lobby are rooms of various sizes, with creamy pastels and dark wood furnishings. The bureau drawers are lined with sheet music, and every room is outfitted with terry-cloth robes, a microwave oven, a minibar, fresh flowers, and a basket of apples. All rooms have queen-size beds, though the standard rooms are a bit cramped. A major attraction is the sumptuous, dimly lighted Act IV restaurant; stars congregate here before and after performances. ⊠ *333 Fulton St., 94102,* ☎ *415/863−8400 or 800/325−2708; 800/423−9610 in CA;* 𝔽𝔸𝕏 *415/861−0821. 48 rooms. Restaurant, lobby lounge, room service, concierge, parking (fee). AE, DC, MC, V.*

$$$ ⊡ **The Mansions.** An arresting combination of elegance and eccentricity, the Mansions is both lavish and a lark. Fresh flowers and antique furniture decorate the sumptuous

rooms, which vary in theme from the tiny Tom Thumb room to the grand Presidential and Josephine suites (the latter a favorite of Barbra Streisand); most overlook a rose and sculpture garden. Housed in a twin-turreted 1887 Queen Anne, the hotel's minimuseums display historic documents, magic memorabilia, and—as an indulgence to resident ghost Claudia's predilection for pigs—various "porkabilia." Rates include a full breakfast and a campy magic show. ✉ *2220 Sacramento St., 94115,* ☏ *415/929–9444,* ℻ *415/567–9391. 26 rooms. Breakfast room, dining room, billiards, laundry service, parking (fee). AE, DC, MC, V.*

$$$ 🏨 **Radisson Miyako Hotel.** Near the Japantown complex and not far from Fillmore Street and Pacific Heights, this pagoda-style hotel is popular with business travelers, especially those from Japan. Rooms are in the tower building and the garden wing, which has traditional gardens. Japanese-style rooms have futon beds with tatami mats, while Western rooms have traditional beds—but all feature gorgeous Asian furniture and original artwork. Most have their own soaking rooms with a bucket and stool and a Japanese tub (1 ft deeper than Western tubs). In-room shiatsu massages are available. ✉ *1625 Post St., at Laguna St., 94115,* ☏ *415/922–3200 or 800/533–4567,* ℻ *415/921–0417. 218 rooms. Restaurant, bar, exercise room, laundry service and dry cleaning, business services. AE, D, DC, MC, V.*

$$ 🏨 **The Abigail.** This hotel, a former B&B, retains its distinctive atmosphere with an eclectic mix of faux-stone walls, a faux-marble front desk, and an old-fashioned telephone booth in the lobby. Hissing steam radiators, down comforters, and antiques complete the mood. The new Millennium Restaurant serves food so delicious it's hard to believe it's vegan (no meat or dairy). ✉ *246 McAllister St., 94102,* ☏ *415/861–9728 or 800/243–6510,* ℻ *415/861–5848. 60 rooms. Restaurant, laundry service. AE, D, DC, MC, V.*

$$ 🏨 **Phoenix Hotel.** From the piped-in, poolside jungle music to the libations in the ultrahip Backflip lounge across the courtyard, the Phoenix evokes the tropics—or at least a fun, kitschy version of it. It's not the place for an executive seeking serenity—or anyone put off by its location on the fringes of the seedy Tenderloin District—but then it does attract celebrities, including bands R.E.M. and Pearl Jam. Rooms are simple, with handmade bamboo furniture, white beamed ceilings, tropical-print bedspreads, and original art. All rooms face the courtyard pool (with a mural by Francis Forlenza on its bottom) and sculpture garden. ⊠ *601 Eddy St., 94109,* ☎ *415/776–1380 or 800/248–9466,* FAX *415/885–3109. 44 rooms. Restaurant, bar, room service, pool, massage, nightclub, laundry service, free parking. AE, D, DC, MC, V.*

5 Nightlife and the Arts

NIGHTLIFE

Updated
by Julene
Snyder

San Francisco has a tremendous potpourri of evening entertainment, from ultrasophisticated cabarets to bawdy bistros that reflect the city's gold rush past. Although it's a compact city with the prevailing influences of some neighborhoods spilling into others, the following generalizations should help you find the kind of entertainment you're looking for. **Nob Hill** is noted for its plush piano bars and panoramic skyline lounges. **North Beach,** infamous for its topless and bottomless bistros, has cleaned up its image considerably and yet still maintains a sense of its beatnik past—a legacy that lives on in atmospheric bars and coffeehouses. **Fisherman's Wharf,** although touristy, is great for people-watching and attracts plenty of street performers. Tony **Union Street** is home away from home for singles in search of company. South of Market—**SoMa,** for short—has become a hub of nightlife, with a bevy of highly popular nightclubs, bars, and lounges in renovated warehouses and auto shops. Gay men will find their scene in the **Castro** and on **Polk Street.** Twentysomethings and alternative types should check out the ever-funky **Mission District** and **Haight Street** scenes.

For information on who is performing where, check out the Sunday *San Francisco Examiner/Chronicle*'s pink "Datebook" insert—or consult the *Bay Guardian,* free and available in racks around the city, listing neighborhood, avant-garde, and budget-priced events. *S.F. Weekly* is also free and packed with information on arts events around town. Another handy reference is the weekly magazine *Key,* offered free in most major hotel lobbies and at Hallidie Plaza (Market and Powell streets). For a phone update on musical and cultural events, call the Convention and Visitors Bureau's Events Hotline (☎ 415/391–2001).

With the exception of the hotel lounges and discos noted below, casual dress is the norm. Bars generally close around 2 AM. Bands and other performers usually begin between 8 PM and 11 PM. The cover charge at smaller clubs ranges from $3 to $10, and credit cards are rarely accepted. At the larger venues the cover may go up to $30, and tickets can often be purchased through BASS (☎ 415/776–1999 or 510/762–2277).

Blues, Rock, Pop, and Folk

Bimbo's 365 Club's (✉ 1025 Columbus St., at Chestnut St., ☎ 415/474–0365) large, plush room retains a retro ambience apt for the "Cocktail Nation" programming that keeps the dance floor hopping. Progressive jazz and alternative rock take the stage at this stylish club.

The Blue Lamp (✉ 561 Geary St., ☎ 415/885–1464), a downtown hole-in-the-wall showcasing blues performers, has an aura of faded opulence. Local rock is on the agenda every Friday and Saturday night.

Bottom of the Hill (✉ 1233 17th St., at Texas St., ☎ 415/626–4455), in the Potrero Hill neighborhood, showcases some of the city's best local alternative rock and blues in an ultra low-key atmosphere.

DNA Lounge (✉ 375 11th St., near Harrison St., ☎ 415/626–1409), a longtime, two-floor SoMa haunt, headlines alternative rock, funk, and rap, as well as weekly theme nights: Tuesday industrial and alternative rock; Wednesday reggae, soul, and R&B; Thursday rockabilly. Live bands play on most weekends.

The Fillmore (✉ 1805 Geary Blvd., at Fillmore St., ☎ 415/346–6000), one of San Francisco's most famous rock music halls, serves up a varied menu of national and local acts: rock, reggae, grunge, jazz, comedy, folk, acid house, and more. Avoid steep ticket service charges by buying tickets at the Fillmore box office Sunday 10–4.

Freight and Salvage Coffee House (✉ 1111 Addison St., Berkeley, ☎ 510/548–1761), one of the finest folk houses in the country, is worth a trip across the bay. Talented practitioners of folk, blues, Cajun, and bluegrass perform in this smoke- and alcohol-free space, where tickets range from $8 to $12.

Great American Music Hall (✉ 859 O'Farrell St., between Polk and Larkin Sts., ☎ 415/885–0750) is one of the greatest eclectic nightclubs in the country. You'll find top-drawer performers and pristine sound, with acts running the gamut from blues, folk, and jazz to alternative rock with a sprinkling of comedians. The colorful marble-pillared emporium (built in 1907 as a bordello) also allows dancing at some shows. Pub grub is available most nights.

John Lee Hooker's Boom Boom Room (⊠ 1601 Fillmore St., no phone) is a newcomer in an old-time spot occupying what was formerly Jack's Bar. There's dancing seven nights a week to R&B and blues and live music Thursday through Saturday.

Kilowatt (⊠ 3160 16th St., ☎ 415/861–2595) attracts adventurous indie-rock fans, with an emphasis on loud, cutting-edge acts, both local and national.

Last Day Saloon (⊠ 406 Clement St., between 5th and 6th Aves., ☎ 415/387–6343) hosts major entertainers and rising local bands with a varied schedule of blues, Cajun, rock, and jazz.

Pier 23 (⊠ Embarcadero and Pier 23 across from Fog City Diner, ☎ 415/362–5125), a waterfront restaurant by day, turns into a packed club by night, with a musical spectrum ranging from Caribbean, salsa, and jazz to Motown and reggae.

Slim's (⊠ 333 11th St., ☎ 415/522–0333), one of SoMa's most popular nightclubs, specializes in the cream of the crop in national touring acts—mostly classic rock, blues, and jazz. Co-owner Boz Scaggs helps bring in the crowds and famous headliners.

The Warfield (⊠ 982 Market St., ☎ 415/775–7722), once a movie palace, is one of the city's largest rock-and-roll venues. There are tables and chairs downstairs, and theater seating upstairs.

Cabarets

Club Fugazi (⊠ 678 Green St., ☎ 415/421–4222) is most famous for *Beach Blanket Babylon,* a wacky musical revue that has become the longest-running show of its genre. A send-up of San Francisco moods and mores, *Beach Blanket* has now run for two decades, outstripping the Ziegfeld Follies by years, and even surviving director Steve Silver, who died in 1995. Although the choreography is colorful, the singers brassy, and the songs witty, the real stars are the comically exotic costumes and famous ceiling-high "hats." Order tickets as far in advance as possible; the revue has been sold out up to a month in advance. Those under 21 are admitted only to the Sunday matinee.

Coconut Grove (⊠ 1415 Van Ness Ave., ☎ 415/776–1616) has a chic but whimsical '40s supper-club ambience, along with superb cocktails and nouvelle cuisine. Weeknights bring a '40s menu with '40s prices (prices climb on weekends). There's swing music on Tuesday, ragtime jazz piano Wednesday, and R&B on Thursday; Friday and Saturday bring big band tunes, and Latin salsa follows on Sunday.

Finocchio's (⊠ 506 Broadway, ☎ 415/982–9388), an amiable, world-famous club, has been generating confusion with its female impersonators since 1936. The scene at Finocchio's is decidedly retro, which for the most part only adds to its charm. It's open from Thursday through Saturday.

Josie's Cabaret and Juice Joint (⊠ 3583 16th St., at Market St., ☎ 415/861–7933), a small, stylish café and cabaret in the Castro District, books performers who reflect the countercultural feel of the neighborhood—from stand-up comedians to drag queens to monologuists.

New Orleans Room (⊠ Mason and California Sts., ☎ 415/772–5259), in the Fairmont Hotel, has a somewhat tacky 1960s hotel-bar ambience. Still, the talent on display is first-rate: Recent guests have included actress Cybill Shepherd and Frank Sinatra Jr.

Comedy Clubs

Cobb's Comedy Club (⊠ 2801 Leavenworth St., at Beach St., ☎ 415/928–4320), in the Cannery, books super stand-up comics such as Jake Johannsen, Rick Overton, and Janeane Garofalo.

Punch Line (⊠ 444 Battery St., between Clay and Washington Sts., ☎ 415/397–7573), a launching pad for the likes of Jay Leno and Whoopi Goldberg, features some of the area's top talents. Weekend shows often sell out; buy tickets in advance at BASS outlets (☎ 510/762–2277) or from the club's new charge line (☎ 415/397–4337).

Other comedy possibilities: Josie's (☞ Cabarets, *above*) often books gay comics. The Fillmore and the Great American Music Hall (☞ Blues, Rock, Pop, and Folk *above*) are also apt to have an occasional favorite comic onstage.

Dancing Emporiums

Some of the rock, blues, and jazz clubs listed above have active dance floors. Below are several spots devoted solely to folks out to shake a tail feather.

Cesar's Latin Palace (⊠ 3140 Mission St., ☎ 415/648–6611), in the Mission District, is an alcohol-free club that lures all kinds of dancers with its salsa-style Latin music. Latin dance lessons from 9 to 10 PM are included in the price of admission Friday and Saturday nights. Sunday is Brazilian Night.

El Rio (⊠ 3158 Mission St., ☎ 415/282–3325) is a casual Mission District spot with salsa dancing on Sunday (from 4 PM), '70s soul and funk on Wednesday, a global dance party on Friday, and live rock Saturday and Sunday.

Metronome Ballroom (⊠ 1830 17th St., ☎ 415/252–9000) is at its most lively on weekends, when ballroom, Latin, and swing dancers come for lessons and revelry. The ambience is fun but mellow at this smoke- and alcohol-free spot.

Oz (⊠ 335 Powell St., between Geary and Post Sts., ☎ 415/774–0116), on the top floor of the St. Francis Hotel, has marble floors, cushy sofas, and a splendid panorama of the city. Weekends offer jazz, contemporary, pop, and funk; on Sunday and Monday DJs spin progressive house music and hip-hop over the fine sound system.

Gay and Lesbian Nightlife

In the days before the gay liberation movement, bars also served as community centers where members of a mostly undercover minority could network and socialize. In the 1960s they became hotbeds of political activity: The Tavern Guild of San Francisco achieved several of the community's first political victories. Old-timers may wax nostalgic about the vibrancy of pre-AIDS, '70s bar life, but you can still have plenty of fun today. The one difference is the one-night-a-week operation of some of the best clubs, which may cater to a different (sometimes straight) clientele on other nights.

This type of club tends to come and go, so it's best to call ahead and pick up one of the two main gay papers: the *Bay Area Reporter* (☎ 415/861–5019) or the *San Francisco Bay Times* (☎ 415/227–0800). Both, plus *Frontiers,* a club-info and gossip sheet, are usually available at the clubs listed below. Check these papers for cultural and miscellaneous activities, too.

Lesbian Bars

Younger lesbians and gays don't segregate themselves quite as much as the older set; you'll find mixed crowds at a number of the bars listed under Gay Male Bars, *below.*

Girl Spot (⊠ 401 6th St., ☎ 415/337–4962), affectionately nicknamed the G-Spot, recently moved to SoMa's End Up. Every Saturday night from 9, dance to Top 40, house, and R&B; several top San Francisco DJs keep the mix lively.

The Lexington Club (⊠ 3464 19th St., at Mission St., ☎ 415/863–2052) is a seven-days-a-week bar for frisky young women swaying to the hip and groovy tunes on the jukebox.

Gay Male Bars

Alta Plaza Restaurant & Bar (⊠ 2301 Fillmore St., ☎ 415/922–1444) is an upper Fillmore restaurant-bar that caters to nattily dressed guppies and their admirers. Live jazz is offered Sunday through Thursday nights; a DJ takes over on weekends.

The Café (⊠ 2367 Market St., at 17th St., ☎ 415/861–3846), formerly Café San Marcos, is in the heart of the gay Castro district. Always comfortable and often crowded, this place lets you chat quietly or cut the rug as you please.

The Metro (⊠ 3600 16th St., at Market St., ☎ 415/703–9750) has a balcony that overlooks the intersection of Noe, 16th, and Market streets. Guppies love this place, especially since it has a fairly good restaurant adjoining the bar. Tuesday brings Karaoke Night from 8:30 on.

N Touch (✉ 1548 Polk St., ☎ 415/441–8413), a tiny dance bar, has long been popular with Asian–Pacific Islander gay men. In addition to videos, there's karaoke Tuesday and Sunday nights, and male strippers perform Thursday night. A monthly drag show and go-go dancers on weekends round out the entertainment.

The Stud (✉ Harrison and 9th Sts., ☎ 415/252–7883) in SoMa is still going strong after more than 30 years. Its always-groovin' DJs mix up-to-the-minute music with carefully chosen highlights from the glory days of gay disco. The ever-changing weekly schedule includes new wave, classic disco, funk, and rock. Thursday is the Trannie Shack, a drag cabaret show.

Jazz

There's been a major revival in the local jazz scene, thanks largely to a new generation of local performers like the Broun Fellinis and Charlie Hunter. Check the above-listed Blues, Rock, Pop, and Folk venues for special jazz events.

Bruno's (✉ 2389 Mission St., at 20th St., ☎ 415/550–7455) is a slice of retro heaven in the Mission District. Huge red booths provide a comfy place to ogle the beautiful people ordering swanky cocktails. An excellent menu draws crowds while two lounges attract rotating local jazz, swing, and retro bands.

Cafe du Nord (✉ 2170 Market St., at Sanchez St., ☎ 415/979–6545) hosts some of the coolest jazz, blues, and alternative sounds in town. The atmosphere in this basement poolroom bar is decidedly casual, but the local talent is mostly top-notch.

Enrico's (✉ 504 Broadway, at Kearny St., ☎ 415/982–6223), a beat-era tradition, is hip once again—the indoor/outdoor café has a high-life ambience, a fine menu (tapas and Italian), and mellow nightly jazz combos.

Jazz at Pearl's (✉ 256 Columbus Ave., near Broadway, ☎ 415/291–8255) is sophisticated and romantic, with picture windows overlooking City Lights Bookstore. The talent level is remarkably high, especially considering that there is rarely a cover.

Orocco East-West Supper Club (⊠ 3565 Geary St., at Arguello St., ☎ 415/387–8788) is one of the city's best trendy retro supper clubs. Malaysian chef Alexander Ong oversees a sensational array of East-West hybrid dishes in the restaurant, and there's live mellow jazz Wednesday from 8:30 PM and weekends from 6:30 PM.

Up and Down Club (⊠ 1151 Folsom St., ☎ 415/626–2388), a hip restaurant and club whose owners include supermodel Christy Turlington, books up-and-coming jazz artists downstairs, as well as dancing to a DJ upstairs from Monday through Saturday.

Piano Bars

Act IV Lounge (⊠ 333 Fulton St., near Franklin St., ☎ 415/553–8100), in the Inn at the Opera hotel, is a popular spot for a romantic rendezvous. The focal point of this tastefully appointed, intimate restaurant-lounge is a crackling fireplace.

Club 36 (⊠ 345 Stockton St., ☎ 415/398–1234), on the top floor of the Grand Hyatt, offers piano music and a view of North Beach and the bay.

Redwood Room (⊠ Taylor and Geary Sts., ☎ 415/775–4700), in the Clift Hotel, is a classy art deco lounge with a low-key but sensuous ambience. Klimt reproductions cover the walls, and mellow sounds fill the air.

Ritz-Carlton Hotel (⊠ 600 Stockton St., ☎ 415/296–7465) has a tastefully appointed lobby lounge where a harpist plays during high tea (weekdays 2:30–4:30, weekends 1–4:30). The lounge shifts to piano (with occasional vocal accompaniment) for cocktails until 11:30 weeknights and 1:30 AM weekends.

Washington Square Bar and Grill (⊠ 1707 Powell St., on Washington Sq., ☎ 415/982–8123), affectionately known as the "Washbag" among San Francisco politicians and newspaper folk, hosts pianists performing jazz and popular standards.

San Francisco's Favorite Bars

Locals patronize all of the places we've listed, but there are several joints they hold near and dear.

Buena Vista (⊠ 2765 Hyde St., ☎ 415/474–5044), the wharf area's most popular bar, introduced Irish coffee to the New World—or so they say. It has a fine view of the waterfront.

Cypress Club (⊠ 500 Jackson St., at Columbus Ave., ☎ 415/296–8555) is an eccentric restaurant-bar where sensual, '20s-style opulence clashes with Fellini/Dalí frivolity. The decor alone makes it worth a visit, but it's also a good spot for a before-dinner or after-theater chat. It has live jazz nightly.

Edinburgh Castle (⊠ 950 Geary St., near Polk St., ☎ 415/885–4074), cherished by Scots all over town, pours out happy and sometimes baleful Scottish folk tunes; Friday brings bagpipe performances. You can work off your fish-and-chips and Scottish brews with a turn at the dart board or pool table. There's live music from Wednesday through Saturday nights.

Harrington's (⊠ 245 Front St., ☎ 415/392–7595), a family-owned Irish drinking saloon, is a full-service restaurant serving American fare from Monday through Saturday.

House of Shields (⊠ 39 New Montgomery St., ☎ 415/392–7732), a saloon-style bar with a large wine cellar, attracts an older, Financial District crowd after work. Food is served weekdays until 8; weekends it's closed.

Tonga Room (⊠ 950 Mason St., at California St., ☎ 415/772–5278), for nearly 50 years, has given San Francisco a beloved taste of high Polynesian kitsch from its ecosystem on the Fairmont Hotel's terrace level. Fake palm trees, grass huts, a lake (three-piece combos play pop standards on a floating barge), and sprinkler-system rain—complete with simulated thunder and lightning—create the ambience, which only grows more surreal as you quaff the selection of very fruity, and very potent, novelty cocktails.

Tosca Café (⊠ 242 Columbus Ave., ☎ 415/391–1244), like nearby Vesuvio, holds a special place in San Francisco lore.

It has an Italian flavor, with opera, big band, and Italian standards on the jukebox. Known as a hangout for film-maker Francis Ford Coppola, playwright–actor Sam Shepard, and ballet star Mikhail Baryshnikov (when they're in town), this place positively breathes a film noir atmosphere.

Vesuvio Cafe (⊠ 255 Columbus Ave., between Broadway and Pacific Ave., ☎ 415/362–3370), near the legendary City Lights Bookstore, is little altered since its heyday as a haven for the beat poets. The second-floor balcony is a fine vantage point for watching the colorful, slightly seedy Broadway–Columbus intersection.

Singles Bars

Harry Denton's (⊠ 161 Steuart St., ☎ 415/882–1333), one of San Francisco's liveliest, most upscale saloons, is packed with well-dressed young professionals. There are live bands and dancing after 10 every night except Sunday. Located on the Embarcadero, where the freeway came down after the '89 quake, it's a great place to enjoy stunning views of the bay—especially from the back bar.

Holding Company (⊠ 2 Embarcadero Center, ☎ 415/986–0797), one of the most popular weeknight Financial District watering holes, is where scores of office workers enjoy friendly libations. The kitchen and bar are open weekdays.

Johnny Love's (⊠ 1500 Broadway, at Polk St., ☎ 415/931–8021) menu features American club fare, and live music ranges from ska to swing to rockabilly to reggae. Late-night dancing to DJ-spun modern rock is also an option.

Perry's (⊠ 1944 Union St., at Buchanan St., ☎ 415/922–9022), the most famous of San Francisco's singles bars, is usually jam-packed. You can dine here on great hamburgers as well as more substantial fare.

Skyline Bars

San Francisco is a city of spectacular vistas. Enjoy drinks, music, and sometimes dinner with 360-degree views at any of the bars below.

Carnelian Room (⊠ 555 California St., ☎ 415/433–7500), on the 52nd floor of the Bank of America Building, has what is perhaps the loftiest view of San Francisco's magnificent skyline. Enjoy dinner or cocktails at 779 ft above the ground; reservations are a must for dinner. The dress code requires jackets; ties are optional.

Crown Room (⊠ California and Mason Sts., ☎ 415/772–5131), the aptly named lounge on the 23rd floor of the Fairmont Hotel, is one of the most luxurious of the city's skyline bars. Just riding the glass-enclosed Skylift elevator is an experience in itself.

Equinox (⊠ 5 Embarcadero Center, ☎ 415/788–1234), on the 22nd floor of the Hyatt Regency, is known for its revolving 360-degree views of the city. You can sightsee, eat, and drink, all from the comfort of your own chair.

Harry Denton's Starlight Room (⊠ 450 Powell St., ☎ 415/395–8595), on the 21st floor of the Sir Francis Drake Hotel, re-creates a 1950s high-life tenor with rose-velvet booths, romantic lighting, and staff clad in tuxes or full-length gowns. Whenever live combos playing jazz, standards, and swing aren't holding court over the small dance floor, taped Sinatra rules.

Phineas T. Barnacle (⊠ 1090 Point Lobos Ave., ☎ 415/666–4016), inside the Cliff House, provides a unique panorama of Seal Rock and the horizon of the Pacific Ocean.

Top of the Mark (⊠ California and Mason Sts., ☎ 415/392–3434), in the Mark Hopkins Hotel, hosts live music Wednesday through Saturday nights, and dancing to standards from the '20s, '30s, and '40s on Friday and Saturday.

View Lounge (⊠ 55 4th St., at Market St., ☎ 415/896–1600), in the San Francisco Marriott, is one of the loveliest of the city's skyline lounges. There's live piano music Monday–Wednesday, and live jazz and blues Thursday–Saturday, from 9:30 PM to 1 AM.

Wine Bars

EOS Restaurant and Wine Bar (⊠ 101 Carl St., ☎ 415/566–3064) is a cozy space with hundreds of wines by the bottle and many by the glass. Tastings take place Thursdays at 6:30. The restaurant puts an emphasis on food and wine pairings; expect to find the hard-to-find here.

Hayes and Vine (✉ 377 Hayes St., ☎ 415/626–5301) provides a warm haven defined by a stunning white-onyx underlighted bar, where patrons relax and taste a few of the 550 wines available by the bottle, or the 40 selections served by the glass. The clientele ranges from after-opera visitors to younger wine aficionados.

London Wine Bar (✉ 415 Sansome St., ☎ 415/788–4811) lays claim to the title of first official wine bar in the United States. This warm Financial District spot (open weekdays only) offers 40 wines by the glass from a cellar of 8,000 bottles. Daily tastings by the half glass are available, and a four-wine sampler changes every Monday.

THE ARTS

Updated by Julene Snyder

The best guide to arts and entertainment events in San Francisco is the "Datebook" section, printed on pink paper, in the Sunday *San Francisco Examiner/Chronicle*. Also consult any of the free alternative weeklies (☞ Nightlife, *above*). For up-to-date information about cultural and musical events, call the Convention and Visitors Bureau's Events Hotline (☎ 415/391–2001).

Half-price, same-day tickets to many local and touring stage shows go on sale (cash only) at 11 AM from Tuesday through Saturday at the **TIX Bay Area** booth, on the Stockton Street side of Union Square between Geary and Post streets. TIX is also a full-service ticket agency for theater and music events around the Bay Area (open until 6 Tuesday–Thursday and 7 Friday–Saturday). For recorded information about TIX tickets, call 415/433–7827.

The city's charge-by-phone ticket service is **BASS** (☎ 510/762–2277 or 415/776–1999), with one of its centers in the TIX booth (☞ *above*) and another at Tower Records (✉ Bay St. at Columbus Ave., ☎ 415/885–0500), near Fisherman's Wharf. The **City Box Office** (✉ 153 Kearny St., Suite 402, ☎ 415/392–4400) has a downtown charge-by-phone service for many concerts and lectures. The **Downtown**

Center Box Office (✉ In the parking garage at 325 Mason St., ☎ 415/775–2021) accepts charges for tickets by phone. The opera, symphony, the San Francisco Ballet's *Nutcracker,* and touring hit musicals are often sold out in advance; tickets are usually available within a day of performance for other shows.

Although the city's major commercial theaters are concentrated downtown, the opera, symphony, and ballet traditionally perform at the Civic Center.

Dance

The **San Francisco Ballet** (✉ 301 Van Ness Ave., ☎ 415/865–2000) has regained much of its luster under artistic director Helgi Tomasson, and both classical and contemporary works have won admiring reviews. The company's primary season runs from February through May. Its repertoire includes such full-length ballets as *Swan Lake, Sleeping Beauty,* and a new production of *Romeo and Juliet*; its annual *Nutcracker* is one of the most spectacular in the nation. The company also performs bold new dances from such star choreographers as William Forsythe and Mark Morris, alongside modern classics by Balanchine and Jerome Robbins. Tickets and information are available at the ballet's administration building (✉ 455 Franklin Street, behind the Opera House, ☎ 415/861–5600).

Cal Performances and **San Francisco Performances** (☞ Music, *below*) are the area's leading importers of world-class dance groups.

Approximately 30 of the Bay Area's estimated 200 ethnic dance companies and soloists perform at the **Ethnic Dance Festival** (✉ Palace of Fine Arts Theatre, Bay and Lyon Sts., ☎ 415/474–3914) in June. Prices are modest.

The **Margaret Jenkins Dance Company** (✉ 3973-A 25th St., ☎ 415/826–8399) is a nationally acclaimed modern troupe. **Lines Contemporary Ballet** (✉ 50 Oak St., 4th floor, ☎ 415/863–3040) is a good bet for modern ballet. **ODC/San Francisco** (✉ 3153 17th St., ☎ 415/863–6606) mounts an annual Yuletide version of *The Velveteen Rabbit.* For cutting-edge, experimental work, try the **Joe Goode**

Performance Group (⊠ 3221 22nd St., ☎ 415/648–4848) or **Contraband** (☎ 415/431–9167). The **Robert Henry Johnson Dance Company** (☎ 415/824–4782) mounts contemporary productions, usually at Yerba Buena Center for the Arts and Theatre Artaud.

Film

The San Francisco Bay Area, including Berkeley and San Jose, is considered one of the nation's most important movie markets; films of all sorts find an audience here. The area is also a filmmaking center: Documentaries and experimental works are produced on modest budgets, feature films and television programs are shot on location, and some of Hollywood's biggest directors (including George Lucas and Francis Ford Coppola) live in the city or, more often, in Marin County. In San Francisco about a third of the theaters regularly show foreign and independent films. The city is also one of the last strongholds of repertory cinema (sometimes called revival houses), showing older American and foreign films on bills that change daily.

The **Castro** (⊠ Castro St. near Market St., ☎ 415/621–6120), designed by art deco master Timothy Pfleuger, is worth visiting for its decor alone; it also offers revivals as well as foreign and independent engagements. The pseudo-mosque-styled **Alhambra** (⊠ Polk St. at Union St., ☎ 415/775–2137), another stunning Pfleuger-designed theater, shows new Hollywood releases.

First-run commercial cinemas are scattered throughout the city, concentrated along Van Ness Avenue near Japantown, at the Embarcadero Center, and in the Marina District. All are accessible on major Muni bus routes, along with the art-revival houses. The San Francisco International Film Festival (☞ *below*), the oldest in the country, provides an extensive selection of foreign films each spring.

Foreign and Independent Films

The **Roxie Cinema** (⊠ 3117 16th St., ☎ 415/863–1087) specializes in Hong Kong action movies, film noir, and new foreign and indie features. The avant-garde **Red Vic Movie House** (⊠ 1727 Haight St., ☎ 415/668–3994) is aimed at twentysomething tastes. The **Cinematheque** (☎ 415/558–

8129) splits its experimental film and video schedule between the San Francisco Art Institute (⊠ 800 Chestnut St., ☎ 415/558–8129) and the Center for the Arts at Yerba Buena Gardens (701 Mission St., between 3rd and Howard Sts., ☎ 415/978–2787). The **Phyllis Wattis Theatre,** at the San Francisco Museum of Modern Art (⊠ 151 3rd St., ☎ 415/357–4000), shows films with an alternative bent.

Other showcases include **Opera Plaza Cinemas** (⊠ Van Ness Ave. at Golden Gate Ave., ☎ 415/352–0810). **Lumière** (⊠ California St. near Polk St., ☎ 415/352–0810). **Clay** (⊠ Fillmore and Clay Sts., ☎ 415/352–0810). **Bridge** (⊠ 3010 Geary Blvd., near Masonic Ave., ☎ 415/751–3212). **Embarcadero Center Cinemas** (⊠ 1 Embarcadero, Promenade level, ☎ 415/352–0810).

Festivals

The **San Francisco International Film Festival's** (☎ 415/931–3456) schedule of about 150 films from around the globe takes over several theaters for two weeks in late April, primarily at the AMC Kabuki complex at Post and Fillmore streets. Marin County's **Mill Valley Film Festival** (☎ 415/383–5256), in early October, is also renowned.

The June **San Francisco Lesbian and Gay International Film Festival** (various venues, ☎ 415/703–8650) is the world's oldest and largest of its kind. The **Jewish film festival** takes place in July (☎ 510/548–0556). In March look for the **Asian American film festival** (☎ 415/863–0814). The documentary-oriented **Film Arts Festival** (☎ 415/552–8760) is in November.

Music

San Francisco Symphony. The symphony performs from September through May under director Michael Tilson Thomas, who is known for his innovative programming of 20th-century American works. Summers include a festival built around a particular composer, nation, or musical period, and Pops Concerts at various venues. Throughout the season the symphony presents a Great Performers Series of guest soloists and orchestras. Tickets run $10–$70. ⊠ *Davies Symphony Hall, Van Ness Ave. at Grove St., ☎ 415/864–6000.*

Berkeley Symphony Orchestra. This East Bay ensemble has risen to considerable prominence under artistic director Kent Nagano's baton. The emphasis is on 20th-century composers from Messiaen to Zappa (including many world premieres), alongside more traditional pieces. The season runs from August through June, with programs every few months. ⊠ *Zellerbach Hall, Telegraph Ave. and Bancroft Way, Berkeley,* ☎ *510/841–2800.*

Cal Performances. This 90-year-old series, running from August through June, offers the Bay Area's most varied bill of internationally acclaimed artists in all disciplines, from classical soloists to the latest jazz, world music, theatre, and dance ensembles. ⊠ *Zellerbach Hall, Telegraph Ave. and Bancroft Way, Berkeley,* ☎ *510/642–9988.*

San Francisco Performances. San Francisco's equivalent to Cal Performances brings an eclectic array of topflight global music and dance talents to various venues—mostly Civic Center's Herbst Theatre—from October through May. ☎ *415/392–4400.*

Philharmonia Baroque. This ensemble is the nation's preeminent group for performances of early music. Its season of concerts, from fall through spring, celebrates composers of the 17th and 18th centuries, including Handel, Vivaldi, and Mozart. ☎ *415/391–5252.*

San Francisco Chamber Symphony. This group is known for the variety of its programming, which includes composers from Handel to Villa-Lobos. ☎ *415/495–2919.*

Kronos Quartet. This surprisingly avant-garde group debunks all conceptions of string quartets as somber affairs with its 20th-century works and premieres. ☎ *415/731–3533.*

Old First Concerts. This Friday evening and Sunday afternoon series of chamber music, vocal soloists, new music, and jazz is well respected. Call for tickets or visit the TIX booth in Union Square (☞ *above*). ⊠ *Old First Presbyterian Church, Van Ness Ave. at Sacramento St.,* ☎ *415/474–1608.*

Stern Grove. The nation's oldest continual free summer music festival hosts Sunday afternoon performances of symphony, opera, jazz, pop music, and dance. The amphitheater is in a eucalyptus grove below street level; dress for cool weather. ⊠ *Sloat Blvd. at 19th Ave.,* ☎ *415/252–6252.*

42nd Street Moon Productions produces delightful "semi-staged" revivals of rare chestnuts from Broadway's musical comedy golden age at the **New Conservatory Theatre Center** (⊠ 25 Van Ness Ave., ☎ 415/861–8972) in irregularly scheduled miniseasons.

Theater

San Francisco's theater row is a single block of Geary Street west of Union Square, but a number of commercial theaters are within walking distance, along with resident companies that enrich the city's theatrical scene. The three major theaters are operated by the Shorenstein-Nederlander organization, which books touring plays and musicals, some before they open on Broadway. The most venerable commercial theater is the **Curran** (⊠ 445 Geary St., ☎ 415/474–3800). The **Golden Gate** is a stylishly refurbished movie theater (⊠ Golden Gate Ave. at Taylor St., ☎ 415/474–3800), now primarily a musical house. The 2,500-seat **Orpheum** (⊠ 1192 Market St., near the Civic Center, ☎ 415/474–3800) is used for the biggest touring shows.

Marines Memorial Theatre (⊠ Sutter and Mason Sts., ☎ 415/441–7444) offers touring shows plus some local performances. The **Stage Door Theater** (⊠ 420 Mason St., no phone) is small but dependable. **Theatre on the Square** (⊠ 450 Post St., ☎ 415/433–9500) is a popular smaller venue. For commercial and popular success, nothing beats *Beach Blanket Babylon,* the zany revue at **Club Fugazi** (⊠ 678 Green St., North Beach, ☎ 415/421–4222) (☞ Cabarets *in* Nightlife, *above*).

The city's major nonprofit theater company is the **American Conservatory Theater (ACT),** one of the nation's leading regional theaters. During its season from approximately October through late spring, ACT presents plays, from classics to contemporary works, often in rotating repertory. Its ticket office is at 405 Geary Street (☎ 415/749–2228). Next door to ACT is its home, the **Geary Theater.**

The leading producer of new plays is the **Magic Theatre** (⊠ Bldg. D, Fort Mason Center, Laguna St. at Marina Blvd, ☎ 415/441–8822). Once Sam Shepard's favorite showcase, the Magic now presents works by the latest rising American playwrights, such as Octavio Solis, Jon Robin Baitz, and Claire Chafee.

The **Lorraine Hansberry Theatre** (⊠ 620 Sutter St., ☎ 415/474–8800) specializes in plays by black writers. The **Asian American Theatre** (☎ 415/440–5545) is dedicated to working with local actors. **A Traveling Jewish Theatre** (⊠ 2800 Mariposa St., ☎ 415/399–1809) stages various productions, often with Jewish themes. **Theatre Rhinoceros** (⊠ 2926 16th St., ☎ 415/861–5079) showcases gay and lesbian performers. **Josie's Cabaret & Juice Joint** (☞ Cabarets, *above*) is a relaxed venue for gay and lesbian works. **BRAVA!** fosters work by women playwrights and directors (⊠ 2789 24th St., ☎ 415/647–2822). The **San Francisco Shakespeare Festival** offers free performances on summer weekends in Golden Gate Park (☎ 415/422–2222). A uniquely Bay Area summertime freebie is the **San Francisco Mime Troupe,** whose politically left, barbed satires are hardly mime in the Marcel Marceau sense; they perform afternoon shows at area parks from July 4 weekend through September (☎ 415/285–1717).

Two animal-free, acrobatically inclined new-vaudeville-style groups offer excellent family shows. **Make-A-Circus** (☎ 415/242–1414), which tours to statewide parks and rec centers in the summer, invites kids to learn circus skills at intermission, then join in during the second act. **The New Pickle Circus** (☎ 415/544–9344) generally performs at indoor locales around Christmas.

Avant-garde theater, dance, opera, and performance art turn up in a variety of locations. The major presenting organization is **Theater Artaud** (⊠ 450 Florida St., between Harrison and Bryant Sts. in the Mission District, ☎ 415/621–7797), which is in a huge, converted machine shop. Some contemporary theater events, in addition to dance and music, are scheduled at the theater in the **Center for the Arts at Yerba Buena Gardens** (⊠ 3rd and Howard Sts., ☎ 415/978–2787). Notable venues for small-scale plays and experimental works include **George Coates Performance Works** (✉ 110 McAllister St., ☎ 415/863–4130), **Intersection for the Arts** (✉ 446 Valencia St., ☎ 415/626–2787), the **Marsh** (✉ 1062 Valencia St., ☎ 415/641–0235), and **Climate Theatre** (✉ 252 9th St., ☎ 415/978–2345). Solo performers are a local staple and are annually spotlighted at the early fall **Solo Mio Festival,** which takes place at various venues (for information call Climate Theatre). The late-summer **Afro Solo Festival** (☎ 415/346–9344) presents solo African-American performers at various locations.

Opera

San Francisco Opera. Founded in 1923 and the resident company at the War Memorial Opera House in the Civic Center since it was built in 1932, the Opera has expanded its fall season to 13 weeks. Approximately 70 performances of 10 operas are given, beginning on the first Friday after Labor Day. The Opera uses supertitles: Translations are projected above the stage during almost all non-English operas. Long considered a major international company and the most important operatic organization in the United States outside New York, the Opera frequently embarks on coproductions with European opera companies. Watch for the occasional summer festival. ✉ *199 Grove St., at Van Ness Ave.,* ☎ *415/864–3330.*

Pocket Opera. This lively, modestly priced alternative to grand opera gives concert performances, mostly in English, of popular and seldom heard works. Offenbach's operettas are frequently on the bill during the February–June season. Concerts are held at various locations. ☎ *415/575–1102.*

Lamplighters. These performers specialize in Gilbert and Sullivan productions, but present other light operas as well. ✉ *Lindland Theatre, Riordan High School, 175 Phelan Ave.,* ☎ *415/227–0331.*

Spoken Word

Check the listings section of the free alternative weekly papers and the Sunday *San Francisco Chronicle/Examiner* "Book Review" section for more exhaustive options.

City Arts and Lectures (☎ 415/392–4400) hosts more than 50 fascinating conversations a year, mostly with literary artists. Events are usually held at the Herbst Theatre (⊠ 401 Van Ness Ave.).

A Clean Well-Lighted Place for Books (⊠ 601 Van Ness Ave., ☎ 415/567–6876) features free author readings and signings four to five times a week, ranging from literary figures to celebrities such as Cindy Crawford and Roger Ebert.

Luna Sea (⊠ 2940 16th St., No. 216C, at S. Van Ness Ave., ☎ 415/863–2989), a gallery and theater space amid the burgeoning Mission District arts scene, has an ever-changing lineup of women's projects, visual arts displays, performances, and readings. Some events are for women only. The space is smoke- and alcohol-free.

6 Outdoor Activities and Beaches

OUTDOOR ACTIVITIES

By Casey
Tefertiller

Updated
by Tara
Duggan

Perhaps more than anywhere else, physical fitness and outdoor activities are a way of life in the Bay Area. Joggers, bicyclists, and aficionados of virtually all sports can often find their favorite pastimes within walking distance of downtown hotels. Golden Gate Park has numerous paths for runners, strollers, in-line skaters, and cyclists. Hiking paths with incredible ocean and bay views are abundant throughout the Golden Gate National Recreation Area (☎ 415/556–0560), which encompasses the San Francisco coastline, the Marin Headlands, and Point Reyes National Seashore. Lake Merced in San Francisco is the most popular area for joggers. Even if you're taking a break from being a tourist, the jogging, biking, and skating routes described below will take you through fun areas to explore.

For a listing of tournaments, races, and other participant sports, check the monthly issues of *City Sports* magazine, available free at sporting goods stores, tennis centers, and other recreational sites.

Bicycling

With its legendary hills, the city offers countless cycling challenges—but also plenty of level ground. To avoid the former, look for a copy of the *San Francisco Biking/Walking Guide* ($3): Sold in select bookstores, the guide indicates street grades and delineates biking routes that avoid major hills and heavy traffic. The number of Bay Area cyclists is reflected in the enormous number of bike shops. Those offering rentals are strategically placed near favorite routes.

EMBARCADERO

A completely flat route, the Embarcadero gives you a clear view of open waters and the Bay Bridge on the pier side and sleek high-rises on the other. Rent a bike at **Start to Finish** (✉ 599 2nd St., ☎ 415/243–8812) and ride downhill on Brannan Street to the Embarcadero. After crossing the Embarcadero, make a left and continue along the waterfront on the sidewalk, along with fellow bikers, joggers, and striders. After passing the Ferry Building, keep pedaling for about a mile to reach Pier 39. If you're not put off by crowds, continue through Fisherman's Wharf to Aquatic

Park. On your return trip continue along the Embarcadero past Brannan Street for additional dockside views. Travel time can be anywhere from 30 minutes to an hour.

MARINA GREEN

The Marina Green is a popular patch of grass along Marina Boulevard adjacent to Fort Mason and the small craft marina. It's also the starting point of a well-trodden route to the Golden Gate Bridge and beyond. Rent a bike at the Lombard branch of **Start to Finish** (⊠ 2530 Lombard St., at Divisadero St., ☎ 415/202–9830) and take Lombard west for three blocks until you reach the Presidio and hit Lincoln Boulevard. Lincoln will eventually bring you to the base of the bridge, a 45-minute ride round-trip. If you're feeling ambitious, head across the bridge (signs indicate on which side cyclists must ride) and turn off on the first road leading northeast. After a 15-minute (downhill) ride, you'll arrive on Bridgeway in downtown Sausalito, where you can rest in a café. From there take your bike aboard the Red and White Fleet's ferry (the ferry terminal is at the end of Bridgeway) for a half-hour ride back to San Francisco's Fisherman's Wharf.

GOLDEN GATE PARK

Golden Gate Park is a beautiful maze of roads and hidden bike paths, with rose gardens, lakes, waterfalls, museums, horse stables, bison, and ultimately, a spectacular view of the Pacific Ocean. On Sunday John F. Kennedy Drive is closed to motor vehicles, making it a popular and crowded route for those on people-powered wheels. Rent a bike at **Park Cyclery** (⊠ 1749 Waller St., ☎ 415/752–8383) and take a 15- to 20-minute ride down John F. Kennedy Drive to the Great Highway, where land meets ocean. You may extend your ride another couple of miles by turning left, riding a few blocks, and hooking onto a raised bike path that runs parallel to the Pacific, winding through fields of emerald green ice plants and, after 2 mi, leading to Sloat Boulevard and the San Francisco Zoo. If you still feel like riding, make a left at Sloat and follow it a ½ mi to Skyline Boulevard; turn right and continue until you see Lake Merced on your left, approximately a ¼ mi from Sloat. Follow the lake clockwise for another 4½ mi. The entire route is moderately level.

Fishing

Numerous fishing boats leave from San Francisco to go for salmon and halibut outside the bay or striped bass and giant sturgeon within the bay (though heavy pollution in the bay may lower the quality of your catch). Trout fishing is possible at Lake Merced; you can rent rods and boats and buy bait at the **Lake Merced Boating and Fishing Company** (☒ 1 Harding Rd., ☎ 415/753–1101). One-day **licenses,** good for ocean fishing only, are available for $5.75 on the charters. Two sportfishing charters are listed below. Most depart daily from Fisherman's Wharf during the salmon-fishing season, which is from March through October. Reservations are suggested.

Lovely Martha's Sportfishing (☒ Fisherman's Wharf, Berth 3, ☎ 415/871–1691) offers salmon-fishing excursions as well as bay tours.

Wacky Jacky (☒ Fisherman's Wharf, Pier 45, ☎ 415/586– 9800) will take you salmon fishing in a sleek, fast, and comfortable 50-ft boat.

Golf

Golfers can putt to their hearts' content in San Francisco. Call the golf information line (☎ 415/750–4653) to get detailed directions to the city's golf courses and reserve tee times. **Harding** and **Fleming parks** (☒ Harding Rd. and Skyline Blvd., ☎ 415/664–4690) have an 18-hole, par-72 course and a 9-hole executive course, respectively. **Lincoln Park** (☒ 34th and Clement Sts., ☎ 415/221–9911) has an 18-hole, par-68 course. **Golden Gate** (☒ 47th Ave. between Fulton St. and John F. Kennedy Dr., ☎ 415/751–8987) is a 9-holer in Golden Gate Park just above Ocean Beach. **Sharp Park,** in Pacifica (☒ Off Hwy. 1 at Fairway Dr. exit, ☎ 650/359–3380), has 18 holes, par 72. **Glen Eagles Golf Course** (☒ 2100 Sunnydale Ave., ☎ 415/587–2425) is a challenging 9-holer in McLaren Park. The **Presidio Golf Course** (☒ W. Pacific Ave. and Arguello Blvd., ☎ 415/561– 4653), an 18-holer managed by Arnold Palmer's company, opened to the public in 1995 and has been a hit ever since.

In-Line Skating

Golden Gate Park is one of the country's best places for in-line skating, with smooth surfaces, manageable hills, and lush scenery. John F. Kennedy Drive, which extends almost to the ocean, is closed to cars on Sunday, when it seems that the city's entire population skates. Beginners practice stopping, and artistic skaters perform their newest moves to music in the large, flat area between the Conservatory and the de Young Museum. **Skates on Haight** (⊠ 1818 Haight St., ☎ 415/752–8376), near the Stanyan Street entrance to the park, offers free lessons (with a purchase) and rents recreational and speed skates.

For beginners, the paved path along **the Marina** offers a 1½-mi (round-trip) easy route on a flat, well-paved surface, with glorious views of San Francisco Bay. **FTC Sports** (⊠ 1586 Bush St., ☎ 415/673–8363) rents and sells in-line skates and protective gear.

BEACHES

San Francisco's beaches are perfect for romantic sunset strolls, but don't expect to find Waikiki-by-the-Metropolis. Freezing-cold year-round temperatures and treacherous currents make most waters dangerous for swimming, and the beach areas are often foggy; expect crowds on those rare sunny days. On the positive side, San Francisco's beaches are quite clean and have dramatic natural settings, despite the urban areas that surround them. During stormy months beachcombers can stroll along the sand and discover a variety of ocean treasures: glossy agates, jade pebbles, and sea-sculpted roots and branches.

Aquatic Park

Nestled in a quiet cove between the lush hills adjoining Fort Mason, the Municipal Pier, and the crowds at Fisherman's Wharf, Aquatic Park has a tiny but sandy beach with gentle water; the distant sound of bongo drums at Fisherman's Wharf adds to the peaceful mood. Keep an eye out for the swim-capped heads of members of the **Dolphin Club** (☎ 415/441–9329), who come bright and early for a dip in these ice-cold waters every day of the year; an especially large and raucous crowd jumps in on New Year's Day.

Baker Beach

Baker Beach is a local favorite, with gorgeous views of the Golden Gate Bridge, the Marin Headlands, and the bay. Its strong, dangerous waves make swimming dangerous, but the mile-long shoreline is ideal for fishing, building sand castles, or watching sea lions play in the surf. On warm days the entire beach is packed with sunbathers. Look for Baker Beach in the southwest corner of the Presidio, beginning at the end of Gibson Road, which turns off Bowley Street. The beach has picnic tables, grills, and trails that lead all the way to Golden Gate Bridge.

China Beach

China Beach was named for the poor Chinese fishermen who once camped here (though it's sometimes marked on maps as James D. Phelan Beach). From April through October the tiny strip of sand offers swimmers gentle waters as well as changing rooms and showers. It's south of Baker Beach and bordered by the gleaming million-dollar homes of the Seacliff neighborhood.

Ocean Beach

South of the Cliff House, Ocean Beach stretches along the western (ocean) side of San Francisco. Though certainly not the city's cleanest beach, it's wide and sandy, stretching for miles and perfect for a long walk or jog. It's popular with surfers, but swimming is not recommended.

7 Shopping

SHOPPING IN SAN FRANCISCO means much more than driving to the local mall. Scattered among the city's diverse neighborhoods are clusters of all sorts of stores: major department stores, fine fashion boutiques, discount outlets, art galleries, and specialty stores for crafts, vintage items, and more. The *San Francisco Chronicle* and the *San Francisco Examiner* advertise sales; for smaller, innovative shops, check the two free weeklies, the San Francisco *Bay Guardian* and *S.F. Weekly,* which can be found on street corners every Wednesday. Store hours vary slightly, but standard shopping times are between 10 and 5 or 6 Monday–Wednesday, Friday, and Saturday; between 10 and 8 or 9 Thursday; and from noon until 5 Sunday. Stores on and around Fisherman's Wharf often have longer hours in summer.

Updated by Julene Snyder

Major Shopping Districts

The Castro/Noe Valley

Often called the gay capital of the world, the Castro is a major destination for nongay travelers as well. Perhaps best known for its vintage-1922 theater, one of the grandest of its kind, the Castro is also filled with clothing boutiques, home accessory stores, and various specialty stores. Especially notable is **A Different Light,** one of the country's premier gay and lesbian bookstores. **Under One Roof** (⌂ 2362-B Market St., ☎ 415/252–9430), housed in the same building as the Names Project, donates the profits from its home and garden items, gourmet foods, bath products, books, frames, and cards to northern California AIDS organizations.

Just south of Castro on 24th Street, the largely residential Noe Valley is an enclave of gourmet food stores, used record shops, clothing boutiques, and specialty gift stores. At **Panetti's** (⌂ 3927 24th St., ☎ 415/648–2414) you'll find whimsical picture frames, journals, costume jewelry, and more.

Chinatown

The intersection of Grant Avenue and Bush Street marks the gateway to Chinatown; here hordes of shoppers and tourists are introduced to 24 blocks of shops, restaurants, markets, and a nonstop tide of activity. Dominating the neighborhood are the sights and smells of food: crates of bok choy, tanks of live crabs, and hanging whole chickens. Racks of Chinese silks, toy trinkets, colorful pottery, baskets, and carved figurines are displayed in racks on the sidewalks, alongside herb stores that specialize in ginseng and roots. The **Great China Herb Co.** (⊠ 857 Washington St., ☎ 415/982–2195), where they add up the bill on an abacus, is one of the biggest herb stores around.

Embarcadero Center

Five modern towers of shops, restaurants, and offices plus the Hyatt Regency Hotel make up the Embarcadero Center, downtown at the end of Market Street.

Fisherman's Wharf

A constant throng of sightseers crowds Fisherman's Wharf, and with good reason: Pier 39, the Anchorage, Ghirardelli Square, and the Cannery are all here, and each has shops, restaurants, and a festive atmosphere, as well as such outdoor entertainment as musicians, mimes, and magicians. Pier 39 includes an amusement area, a double-deck Venetian carousel, and Underwater World aquarium (☞ Chapter 2). Best of all are the wharf's view of the bay and proximity to the cable car lines, which can take shoppers directly to Union Square.

The Haight

Haight Street is always an attraction for visitors, if only to see the sign at Haight and Ashbury streets—the geographic center of flower power during the 1960s. These days, in addition to ubiquitous tie-dyed shirts, you'll find high-quality vintage clothing, funky jewelry, art from around the world, and reproductions of art deco accessories (☞ Vintage Fashion, Furniture, and Accessories, *below*). Used-book stores are another specialty, along with some of the best used-record stores in the city (☞ Music, *below*).

Jackson Square

Tiny gentrified Jackson Square is home to a dozen or so of San Francisco's finest retail antiques dealers, mostly located in two-story town houses (☞ Antique Furniture and Accessories, *below*). From French and English country antiques to Asian collectibles to Biedermeier, every store has a specialty, and all are appointed like small museums. The shops are along Jackson Street in the Financial District, so a visit will put you very close to the Embarcadero Center and Chinatown.

Japantown

Unlike Chinatown, North Beach, or the Mission, shopping here is done under the roof of the 5-acre **Japan Center** (⊠ Between Laguna and Fillmore Sts. and Geary Blvd. and Post St.). The three-block complex includes an 800-car public garage and three shop-filled buildings. Especially worthwhile are the Kintetsu and Kinokuniya buildings, where shops and showrooms sell cameras, tapes and records, new and old porcelain, pearls, antique kimonos, *tansu* chests (Japanese chests used mainly for storage), paintings, and more.

The Marina District

Chestnut Street, one block north of Lombard Street and stretching from Fillmore to Broderick streets, caters to the shopping whims of Marina District residents. Among the district's standouts, **Lucca Delicatessen** is famous for its handmade ravioli and its huge selection of Italian gourmet goods.

The Mission

Known as one of the city's sunniest neighborhoods, the Mission is also one of its most ethnically diverse, with a large Latino population and a growing contingent of young artists, musicians, and new bohemians. In addition to those with a hunger for inexpensive Mexican food, the area draws bargain shoppers with its many used clothing, furniture, and alternative book stores. Shoppers can unwind with a visit to Mission Dolores, a tour of the murals at Precita Eyes Mural Arts Center, or a cup of coffee at one of a dozen or so cafés.

North Beach

The once largely Italian enclave of North Beach grows smaller each year as Chinatown spreads northward. Sometimes called the city's answer to New York City's Greenwich Village, it is only a fraction of the size, clustered tightly around Washington Square and Columbus Avenue. Most of its businesses are small clothing stores; there are antiques and vintage shops as well. Once the center of the beat movement, North Beach still has a bohemian spirit that's especially apparent at **City Lights,** where the beat poets live on.

Pacific Heights

Fillmore Street between Post Street and Pacific Avenue, and Sacramento Street between Lyon and Maple streets, is where private residences alternate with good bookstores, fine clothing and gift shops, thrift stores, and art galleries. A local favorite is the **Sue Fisher King Company,** whose quality home accessories fit right into this upscale neighborhood.

South of Market

SoMa generally has the lowest prices. Dozens of discount outlets, most open daily, have sprung up along the streets and alleyways bordered by 2nd, Townsend, Howard, and 10th streets (☞ Outlets and Discount Stores, *below*). At the other end of the spectrum are the high-class gift shops of the **Museum of Modern Art** and the **Center for the Arts at Yerba Buena Gardens**; both sell handmade jewelry and various other great gift items (☞ Jewelry and Collectibles, *below*).

SoMa's South Park District, or "Multimedia Gulch," as it's known, is one of San Francisco's fastest-growing communities, home to much of the city's computer software industry, and nestled between the 3rd Street offices of *Wired* magazine and the artists' residence known as the Capp Street Project. Within the last few years the area has seen a proliferation of restaurants, designer boutiques, and specialty shops such as **Collections** (✉ 380 Brannan St., ☎ 415/546–9298), where you'll find everything from toys to books to tableware.

Union Square

Serious shoppers head straight to Union Square, San Francisco's main shopping artery and the site of most department stores, including **Macy's, Neiman Marcus,** and **Saks Fifth Avenue** among others. Also here are **F.A.O. Schwarz** and the Disney Store, the Virgin Megastore, and Borders

Books and Music (✉ 400 Post St., ☎ 415/399–1633)
Nearby are the pricey international boutiques of Hermès
of Paris, Gucci, Celine of Paris, Alfred Dunhill, Louis
Vuitton, and Cartier.

The **San Francisco Shopping Centre** (✉ 865 Market St., ☎
415/495–5656), across from the cable car turntable at
Powell and Market streets, is distinguished by spiral escalators that wind up through the sunlit atrium. Inside are
more than 35 retailers, including **Nordstrom,** as well as a
two-floor **Warner Bros.** store (☎ 415/974–5254), with T-
shirts, posters, and other mementos of the studio's past and
present. At Post and Kearny streets, the **Crocker Galleria**
(✉ 50 Post St., ☎ 415/393–1505) is a complex of 40 to
50 shops and restaurants that sit underneath a glass dome.
The rooftop garden has a great vantage point of the busy
streets and sidewalks below.

Union Street

Out-of-towners sometimes confuse Union Street—a popular stretch of shops and restaurants five blocks south of
the Golden Gate National Recreation Area—with downtown's Union Square (☞ *above*). In fact, Union Street is a
tiny, neighborhood version of Union Square. Nestled at the
foot of a hill between Pacific Heights and the Marina District, the street is lined with contemporary fashion and
custom jewelry shops, along with a few antiques shops and
art galleries.

Department Stores

Since San Francisco's department stores are almost all in
shopping centers—Union Square, the San Francisco Shopping Centre, the 660 Center, and Yerba Buena Square—shoppers can hit all the major players without going from one
end of town to the other.

Gump's (✉ 135 Post St., ☎ 415/982–1616), in business
since 1861, is famous for its Christmas window displays
and high-quality collectibles. One of the city's most popular stores for bridal registries, Gump's carries exclusive lines
of dinnerware, flatware, and glassware, as well as Asian
artifacts, antiques, and furniture.

Macy's (⊠ Stockton and O'Farrell Sts., ☎ 415/397–3333) is a one-stop shop, with designer fashions and an extensive array of shoes, housewares, furniture, and food. The men's department—one of the world's largest—occupies its own building across Stockton Street.

Neiman Marcus (⊠ 150 Stockton St., ☎ 415/362–3900), with its Philip Johnson–designed checkerboard facade, gilded atrium, and stained-glass skylight, provides one of the most luxurious shopping experiences in the city. Although its high-end prices raise an eyebrow or two, its biannual "Last Call" sales—in January and July—draw a crowd.

Nordstrom (⊠ 865 Market St., ☎ 415/243–8500), the store that's known for service, is housed in a stunning building with spiral escalators circling a four-story atrium. Designer fashions, shoes, accessories, and cosmetics are specialties.

Saks Fifth Avenue (⊠ 384 Post St., ☎ 415/986–4300) feels like an exclusive, multilevel mall with designer boutiques. With its extensive lines of cosmetics and jewelry, this branch of the New York–based store caters mostly to women, though there is a small men's department on the fifth floor.

Outlets and Discount Stores

A number of factory outlets in San Francisco offer clothing at bargain prices. Outlet maps are available at some of these locations for a nominal fee.

Christine Foley (⊠ 430 9th St., ☎ 415/621–8126) offers discounts of up to 50% on sweaters for men, women, and children. In the small storefront showroom, pillows, stuffed animals, and assorted knickknacks sell at retail prices.

Designer Co-op (⊠ 689 3rd St., ☎ 415/777–3570) sells men's and women's designer clothing at 40%–60% below retail price. Nina K., Armani, Peter Perrino, and Kimbaks are among the names represented. There's also a nice selection of jewelry, accessories, and gift items.

Esprit (⊠ 499 Illinois St., at 16th St., south of China Basin, ☎ 415/957–2550), a San Francisco–based company, manufactures hip sportswear, shoes, and accessories, primarily for young women and children. In a building as big as an airplane hangar, its bare-bones glass-and-metallic interior feels somewhat sterile, but discounts of 30%–70% keep customers happy.

Loehmann's (⊠ 222 Sutter St., near Union Sq., ☎ 415/982–3215), with its drastically reduced designer labels—including Lagerfeld and Krizia—is for fashion-conscious bargain hunters. Labels are often removed, but savvy shoppers will find astounding bargains.

New West (⊠ 426 Brannan St., at 3rd St., ☎ 415/882–4929) specializes in top-notch merchandise for both men and women, including Prada and Jil Sander, at drastic discounts—sometimes up to 50%.

Tower Records Outlet (⊠ 660 3rd St., ☎ 415/957–9660), the city's most prolific record chain, has a crowded outlet with new and used CDs, videotapes, computer books, games, and magazines at discount prices.

Specialty Stores

Antique Furniture and Accessories

The most obvious place to look for antiques is Jackson Square but there are a handful of miscellaneous antiques stores in almost every shopping neighborhood.

Asakichi Japanese Antiques (⊠ 1730 Geary Blvd., ☎ 415/921–2147) carries antique blue-and-white Imari porcelains and handsome tansu chests. Upstairs, **Shige Antique Kimonos** (⊠ 1730 Webster St., on Webster St. Bridge between Kinokuniya and Kintetsu Bldgs., ☎ 415/346–5567) has antique hand-painted, silk-embroidered kimonos as well as cotton *yukatas* (lightweight summer kimonos), obis (sashes worn with kimonos), and other kimono accessories.

Dragon House (⊠ 455 Grant Ave., ☎ 415/781–2351; ⊠ 315 Grant Ave., ☎ 415/421–3693), unlike many other Chinatown stores that peddle cheap reproductions of Chinese art, sells genuine antiques and fine arts. Its collection of ivory carvings, ceramics, and jewelry dates back 2,000 years and beyond—a fact that's especially evident in their prices. The shop's display window is a history lesson in itself.

Hunt Antiques (✉ 478 Jackson St., ☎ 415/989–9531) feels like an English town house, with fine 17th- to 19th-century period English furniture, porcelains, Staffordshire pottery, prints, clocks, and paintings. In the heart of Jackson Square, Hunt is surrounded by other worthwhile shops.

Origins (✉ 680 8th St., ☎ 415/252–7089), in SoMa's Baker Hamilton Square complex, imports unusual collector's items, Chinese furniture, porcelain, silk, and jade; antiques here are up to 400 years old.

Telegraph Hill Antiques (✉ 580 Union St., ☎ 415/982–7055), a tiny North Beach shop, stocks paintings and diverse objets d'art, including crystal, cut glass, Victoriana, and bronzes. Among the store's collection of fine china is a nice selection of Wedgwood pieces.

A Touch of Asia (✉ 1784 Union St., ☎ 415/474–3115) is full of high-end 19th- and 20th-century Asian antiques, mainly from Japan and Korea. Elm and cherrywood furniture, curio cabinets, and chests dominate; the store also carries Asian sculptures, prints and paintings, and antique vases.

Art Galleries

Like small specialty stores, art galleries are ubiquitous in San Francisco. Most surround downtown Union Square, although in recent years some have set up shop in the Hayes Valley area, near the Civic Center and South of Market. Pick up a copy of the free *San Francisco Arts Monthly* at the TIX Bay Area booth in Union Square (✉ Stockton St. at Geary St., ☎ 415/433–7827) for listings of other galleries. Most galleries are closed on Monday.

Art Options (✉ 372 Hayes St., ☎ 415/252–8334), which shares space with Images (☞ *below*), specializes in contemporary glass crafts and one-of-a-kind nonprecious jewelry from local and nationally known artists. A wide variety of affordable art pieces are available.

Hespe Gallery (✉ 1764 Union St., ☎ 415/776–5918) is filled with paintings and drawings by emerging Bay Area artists. Styles include figurative, abstract, and realist. Owner Charles Hespe is an instantly likable art enthusiast who equally delights buyers and browsers.

Images (⊠ 372 Hayes St., ☎ 415/626–2284) specializes in oil paintings and watercolors by northern California realist and impressionist artists.

Keane Eyes Gallery (⊠ 3036 Larkin St, ☎ 415/922–9309) features paintings of the huge-eyed waifs that haunted the '50s. You can purchase posters, plates, note cards, limited-edition prints, and figurines of the little darlings, along with considerably more pricey oils.

San Francisco Women Artists Gallery (⊠ 370 Hayes St., ☎ 415/552–7392), a nonprofit organization, is run and staffed by the women whose work is exhibited. The SFWA displays sculptures, paintings, mixed-media pieces, and video installations. All works are juried, and prices are low.

Vorpal Gallery (⊠ 393 Grove St., ☎ 415/397–9200), a nationally acclaimed gallery with a sister store in New York, carries old and new masters (Rembrandt and Picasso, for example), as well as contemporary and Latin American art and works by emerging artists.

Booksellers

In addition to most major chains, countless small specialty bookstores delight bibliophiles. Most are near other attractions, which makes browsing a convenient and popular pastime.

Alexander Book Co. (⊠ 50 2nd St., at Market St., ☎ 415/495–2992), with three floors of titles, is particularly well stocked with literature and poetry as well as children's books.

Booksmith (⊠ 1644 Haight St., at Clayton St., ☎ 415/863–8688) recently celebrated its 20th anniversary. Come here for current releases, children's titles, and unusual literary finds.

City Lights (⊠ 261 Columbus Ave., ☎ 415/362–8193), the city's most famous and historically interesting bookstore, is where the beat renaissance of the 1950s was born and raised. Best known for poetry, contemporary literature and music, and translations of Third World literature, City Lights also carries books on nature, the outdoors, and travel. An entire room is devoted to poetry. Many titles are published in-house.

A Clean Well-Lighted Place for Books (⊠ 601 Van Ness Ave., ☎ 415/441–6670), in the Opera Plaza, is a great place to browse before or after a performance. Paperback literature and books on opera and San Francisco history are particularly well stocked, but the store bills itself as carrying "a large selection of paperbacks and hardbacks in all fields for all ages."

A Different Light (⊠ 489 Castro St., ☎ 415/431–0891), San Francisco's most extensive gay and lesbian bookstore, has a wide spectrum of books by, for, and about lesbians, gay men, bisexuals, and the transgendered. This is the Castro's unofficial community center. Book signings and readings take place several times each week.

Green Apple Books (⊠ 506 Clement St., ☎ 415/387–2272), a favorite since 1967, has a large used-book department as well as new books in every field. Specialties are comic books, a history room, and a rare-books collection. A new fiction annex is two doors down.

Kinokuniya Bookstore (⊠ Kinokuniya Bldg., 2nd floor, 1581 Webster St., ☎ 415/567–7625), in the Japan Center, may have the finest selection of English-language books on Japanese subjects in the United States. A major attraction is the beautifully produced graphics and art books.

Modern Times Bookstore (⊠ 888 Valencia St., ☎ 415/282–9246) carries quality literary fiction and nonfiction, much of it with a political bent. It also has a Spanish-language section and a wide variety of magazines. Author readings and public forums are held on a regular basis.

Children's Clothing

Dottie Doolittle (⊠ 3680 Sacramento St., ☎ 415/563–3244) is where Pacific Heights mothers buy Florence Eiseman dresses for their little girls and other traditional clothes for boys and girls, from infants to age 14.

Mudpie (⊠ 1694 Union St., ☎ 415/771–9262; ⊠ 2220 Chestnut St., ☎ 415/474–8395) is a treasure chest overflowing with unique children's special-occasion wear such as velvet dresses and handmade booties. Quilts, toys, books, and overstuffed child-size furniture make this a fun store for browsing. The Chestnut branch's clothing is for tots two years old and under.

Small Frys (⊠ 4066 24th St., ☎ 415/648–3954), in the heart of Noe Valley, carries a complete range of colorful cottons for infants and older children, including Oshkosh and California labels.

Clothing for Men and Women

True to its reputation as the most European of American cities, San Francisco is sprinkled liberally with small clothing stores that sell clothes by local designers.

Bella Donna (⊠ 539 Hayes St., ☎ 415/861–7182) offers more than just owner Justine Kaltenbach's self-designed hats; the oversize creations of New York's J. Morgan Puitt, Los Angeles's Kevin Simon, and other top designers make this shop a Hayes Valley treasure. The upstairs loft stocks only bridal garments.

Designers Club (⊠ 3899 24th St., ☎ 415/648–1057), in Noe Valley, specializes in local and national designers who use natural fibers and luxurious fabrics. In addition to clothing, there's a wide selection of hats and handbags.

Justine (⊠ 3600 Sacramento St., ☎ 415/921–8548) is for Francophiles, with women's clothes by French designers Dorothée Bis, Georges Rech, and Fabrice Karel.

North Beach Leather (⊠ 190 Geary St., ☎ 415/362–8300) is one of the city's best sources for high-quality leather garments and accessories. The store, with its wavy wrought-iron banisters, is itself a work of art.

Rolo (⊠ 2351 Market St., ☎ 415/431–4545; ⊠ 450 Castro St., ☎ 415/626–7171; ⊠ 1301 Howard St., ☎ 415/861–1999; ⊠ 21 Stockton St., ☎ 415/989–7656) is a San Francisco favorite, with men's and women's designer denim, sportswear, shoes, and accessories that reveal a distinct European influence.

Solo (⊠ 1599 Haight St., ☎ 415/621–0342) is an opulent space with luxurious women's clothing, much of it from the in-house label, Cornelia. One-of-a-kind pieces, custom work, and hard-to-fit sizes are offered along with jewelry, hats, and scarves.

Worldware (⊠ 336 Hayes St., at Franklin St., ☎ 415/487–9030) is perhaps San Francisco's most ecologically correct store, featuring men's, women's, and children's clothing made from organic hemp, wool, or cotton. It also carries a potpourri of essential oils, skin care products, and aromatherapy candles, as well as antique Americana furniture.

Gourmet Food

Joseph Schmidt Confections (⊠ 3489 16th St., ☎ 415/861–8682) may not be the city's most famous chocolatier (Ghirardelli wins the prize), but it *is* the most gourmet. Its egg-shape truffles, in more than 30 flavors, are the best-selling product, but Schmidt's real specialty is its stunning array of edible, often seasonal, sculptures ranging from chocolate windmills to life-size chocolate turkeys. The unique line of creme-filled chocolate rounds called "slicks" is worth trying.

Just Desserts (⊠ 248 Church St., ☎ 415/626–5774; ⊠ 1000 Cole St., ☎ 415/664–8947; ⊠ 3 Embarcadero Center, ☎ 415/421–1609; ⊠ 836 Irving St., ☎ 415/681–1277; ⊠ 3735 Buchanan St., ☎ 415/922–8675), a Bay Area favorite, carries chocolate velvet mousse cake, almond-flavored chocolate-chip blondies, and other deadly sins.

Lucca Delicatessen (⊠ 2120 Chestnut St., ☎ 415/921–7873) is a bit of old Italy in the upscale Marina District. Choose from among several imported olive oils, a multitude of homemade pastas and Italian sausages, and a wide selection of imported cheeses and prepared salads. A small but respectable wine selection and jars of gourmet delicacies also beckon.

Molinari Delicatessen (⊠ 373 Columbus Ave., ☎ 415/421–2337), billing itself as the oldest delicatessen west of the Rockies, has been making its own salami, sausages, and cold cuts since 1896. Other homemade specialties include meat and cheese ravioli, tortellini with prosciutto filling, homemade tomato sauces, and fresh pastas.

Handicrafts and Folk Art

One lucky consequence of San Francisco's many-layered ethnic mix is that small galleries all over the city sell crafts from all over the world.

The Americas (⊠ 1977 Union St., ☎ 415/921–4600) is a colorful haven with Pueblo and Navajo pottery, Day of the

Dead artifacts, Zuni fetishes, and wood carvings from Oaxaca among the vast selection.

Anokhi (⊠ 1864 Union St., ☎ 415/922–4441), small and inviting, stocks clothing, home furnishings, and accessories from India, with fabrics block-printed by hand in Jaipur. You'll also find Indian tea caddies, scarves, and sarongs, as well as some locally made pottery.

Collage (⊠ 1345 18th St., ☎ 415/282–4401), a studio gallery in Potrero Hill, carries the work of 80 Bay Area artists, including mosaic mirrors, earthquake-proof paper vessels, handblown glass objects, handmade jewelry, and more.

Evolution (⊠ 271 9th St., ☎ 415/861–6665) carries an unusual selection of furniture from Indonesia and pillows from Turkey.

F. Dorian (⊠ 388 Hayes St., ☎ 415/861–3191) has cards, jewelry, and crafts from Mexico, Japan, Italy, Peru, Indonesia, the Philippines, Africa, and Sri Lanka, as well as the glass and ceramic works of local artisans.

Folk Art Boretti Amber (⊠ Ghirardelli Sq., 900 N. Point St., ☎ 415/928–3340) has a vast selection of Baltic amber jewelry and Latin American folk art, such as colonial religious art and Oaxacan wood carvings.

Global Exchange (⊠ 3900 24th St., between Noe and Sanchez Sts., ☎ 415/648–8068), a branch of the well-known nonprofit organization, sells handcrafted items from over 40 countries and works directly with village co-operatives and workshops. When you buy a Nepalese sweater, a South African wood carving, or a Pakistani cap, the staff will explain the origin of your purchase.

Ma-Shi'-Ko Folk Craft (⊠ 1581 Webster St., 2nd floor, ☎ 415/346–0748) carries pottery from Japan, including *mashiko*. There are also Japanese masks, antiques, and handcrafted goods.

Soko Hardware (⊠ 1698 Post St., ☎ 415/931–5510), run by the Ashizawa merchant family in Japantown since 1925, specializes in beautifully crafted Japanese gardening and carpentry tools.

Virginia Breier (⊠ 3091 Sacramento St., ☎ 415/929–7173), a colorful gallery of contemporary and traditional North American crafts, represents mostly emerging artists. Every piece in the store is one-of-a-kind, from jewelry to light fixtures to Japanese tansus.

Xanadu (⊠ Ghirardelli Sq., 900 N. Point St., ☎ 415/441–5211) specializes in artifacts and tribal art from Africa, Oceania, Indonesia, and the Americas, with the bulk of the stock coming from west and central Africa. Carved wood statues preside over a selection of utilitarian and ritual objects, including masks, woven baskets, gorgeous tapestries, tribal jewelry, ceramics, and books.

Housewares and Accessories

Abitare (⊠ 522 Columbus Ave., ☎ 415/392–5800), a popular North Beach shop, has an eclectic mix of goods—soaps and bath supplies, candleholders, artsy picture frames, lamps, and one-of-a-kind furniture, artwork, and decorations.

Biordi (⊠ 412 Columbus Ave., ☎ 415/392–8096), a family-run business for 50 years, imports hand-painted pottery directly from Italy—mainly Tuscany and Umbria—and ships it worldwide. Sets can be ordered in any combination, and prices range from $9 per piece to hundreds of dollars.

Fillamento (⊠ 2185 Fillmore St., ☎ 415/931–2224), a Pacific Heights favorite, has three floors of home furnishings—from dinnerware to bedding to bath and baby accessories—in addition to home office products.

Gordon Bennett (⊠ 2102 Union St., ☎ 415/929–1172; ⊠ Ghirardelli Square, ☎ 415/351–1172) carries housewares and ceramics made by local artists. The artfully designed wrought-iron garden sculptures and furniture, garden tools, dried-flower arrangements, and whimsical topiaries will tempt any homemaker.

Juicey Lucy's & the Sample Store (⊠ 703 Columbus Ave., no phone) sells high-end samples (cards, frames, clothing, pillows) from manufacturers' reps at wholesale prices. An equal draw is Lucy's selection of all-organic juice mixtures.

Kris Kelly (⊠ 174 Geary St., ☎ 415/986–8822), though specializing in handmade quilts from China, is primarily known for its linens, as well as its handcrafted tablecloths, bedding, bath accessories, and window treatments.

Maison d'Etre (⊠ 92 South Park, ☎ 415/357–1747; ⊠ 5330 College Ave., Oakland, ☎ 510/658–0698), an upscale SoMa shop, carries eclectic luxury items, including gorgeous wrought-iron light fixtures, luxurious pillows, ornate mirrors, and jewelry.

Scheuer Linen (⊠ 340 Sutter St., ☎ 415/392–2813), a fixture of Union Square for 40 years, draws designers and everyday shoppers with luxurious linens for the bed, the bath, and the dinner table. There is also a wide variety of gifts for the home and the body.

Sue Fisher King Company (⊠ 3067 Sacramento St., ☎ 415/922–7276; ⊠ 375 Sutter St., ☎ 415/398–2894), a cozy shop in Pacific Heights, offers decorative pillows and luxurious throws, Italian dinnerware, fine linens for the bedroom and kitchen, books on gardening and home decoration, and an aromatic mix of soaps, perfumes, and candles.

Z Gallerie (⊠ 2071 Union St., ☎ 415/346–9000; ⊠ 2154 Union St., ☎ 415/567–4891; ⊠ 1465 Haight St., ☎ 415/863–7466; ⊠ 865 Market St., at the San Francisco Shopping Centre, ☎ 415/495–7121; ⊠ Stonestown Galleria, at 19th Ave. and Winston Dr., ☎ 415/664–7891) carries modern home furnishings and accessories: dinnerware, desks, chairs, lamps, and posters.

Jewelry and Collectibles

The Bead Store (⊠ 417 Castro St., ☎ 415/861–7332) has a daunting collection of more than a thousand kinds of beads, including lapis and carnelian stones, Czechoslovakian and Venetian glass, African trade beads, Buddhist and Muslim prayer beads, and Catholic rosaries. Premade silver jewelry is another specialty.

Center for the Arts gift shop (⊠ 701 Mission St., ☎ 415/978–2710, ext. 168), in Yerba Buena Gardens, carries an outstanding line of handmade jewelry, ceramics, and crafts from both regional and national artists, as well as an unusual selection of glass tableware.

Enchanted Crystal (⊠ 1895 Union St., ☎ 415/885–1335) has a large collection of handcrafted glass jewelry, ornaments, and other art pieces. Many of the pieces are crafted by Bay Area artists. The store also has one of the largest natural quartz balls—12 inches in diameter.

Jade Empire (⊠ 832 Grant Ave., ☎ 415/982–4498), one of the many fine jewelry stores in Chinatown, has jade, diamonds, freshwater pearls, beads, porcelain dolls, and lanterns.

San Francisco Museum of Modern Art gift shop (⊠ 151 3rd St., ☎ 415/357–4035) is famous for its exclusive line of watches and jewelry as well as its artists' monographs, Picasso dishes and other dinnerware, children's art-making sets and books, and extensive collection of art books.

Shreve & Co. (⊠ Post St. and Grant Ave., ☎ 415/421–2600), near Union Square, is one of the city's most elegant jewelers and the oldest retail store in San Francisco. Along with eye-popping gems in dazzling settings, the store carries fine giftware, including Baccarat crystal and Limoges porcelain figurines.

Wholesale Jewelers Exchange (⊠ 121 O'Farrell St., ☎ 415/788–2365), with 28 independent jewelers displaying their own merchandise, is the place to find gems and finished jewelry at less-than-retail prices.

Music

Aquarius Records (⊠ 1055 Valencia St., ☎ 415/647–2272) began as *the* punk rock store in the 1970s. The store's swank new Mission District space carries a large selection of dance music and experimental electronics. You'll find indie rock, new music from Japan and Germany, and New Zealand rock, among other things. The vinyl collection is largest, but there are also new and used tapes and CDs.

Recycled Records (⊠ 1377 Haight St., ☎ 415/626–4075), a Haight Street favorite, buys, sells, and trades a vast selection of used records, including classic rock and roll, obscure independent labels, and hard-to-find imports.

Streetlight Records (⊠ 3979 24th St., ☎ 415/282–3550), a Noe Valley staple for 25 years, buys and sells thousands of used CDs, with a vast selection of rock, jazz, soul, and R&B, and plenty of vinyl. A friendly and knowledgeable staff can help you sift through both new and previously owned tunes.

Virgin Megastore (⊠ 2 Stockton St., ☎ 415/397–4525), the new towering monolith of Union Square, has hundreds of listening stations and an extensive laser disc department, as well as a bookstore and a café overlooking Market Street.

Sporting Goods
G & M Sales (⊠ 1667 Market St., ☎ 415/863–2855), a local institution since 1948, has one of the city's best selections of camping gear, with dozens of pitched tents on display. A large selection of outerwear, hiking boots and shoes, ski goods, and an extensive fishing department make this *the* place for gear fanatics.

North Face (⊠ 180 Post St., ☎ 415/433–3223; ⊠ 1325 Howard St., ☎ 415/626–6444), a Bay Area–based company, is famous for its top-of-the-line tents, sleeping bags, backpacks, and outdoor apparel, including stylish Gore-Tex jackets and pants. The Howard Street store, an outlet, sells overstocked and discontinued items along with occasional seconds.

Toys and Gadgets
The **Disney Store** (⊠ 400 Post St., ☎ 415/391–6866; ⊠ Pier 39, ☎ 415/391–4199), with its colorful walls and gargoyle-shape pillars, sells a potpourri of books, toys, clothing, and collectibles such as framed animation cells.

F.A.O. Schwarz (⊠ 48 Stockton St., ☎ 415/394–8700) is every child's dream, with games, stuffed toys, motorized cars, model trains, and more.

Imaginarium (⊠ 3535 California St., ☎ 415/387–9885; ⊠ Stonestown Galleria at 19th Ave. and Winston Dr., ☎ 415/566–4111) manufactures its own learning-oriented games and gadgets and imports European brands rarely found in larger stores.

Mascara Club (⊠ 1408 Haight St., ☎ 415/863–2837) is a fun place to browse and buy quirky gift items such as recycled art objects, Day of the Dead memorabilia, novelty mouse pads, and icons like Curious George.

Scairy Hairy Toy Company's (⊠ 3804 17th St., ☎ 415/864–6543) toy designers Bruce Hilvitz and Flower Frankenstein work behind the counter on wildly whimsical toys for "people old enough to know better." Thrill to the sight of an Elvis impersonator doll, squeeze a Squeaky Tiki Charm, and admire the works of art and prints from local artists.

Sharper Image (⊠ 532 Market St., ☎ 415/398–6472; ⊠ 680 Davis St., at Broadway, ☎ 415/445–6100; ⊠ 900 North Point, Ghirardelli Sq., ☎ 415/776–1443) carries high-end gadgets that bring out the child in everyone. Marvel over five-language translators, super-shock-absorbent tennis rackets, state-of-the-art speaker systems, Walkman-size computers, digital cameras, and more.

Vintage Fashion, Furniture, and Accessories

American Rag (⊠ 1305 Van Ness Ave., ☎ 415/474–5214) stocks a huge selection of new and used men's and women's clothes from the United States and Europe, all in excellent shape. They also carry shoes and accessories such as sunglasses, hats, belts, and scarves.

Another Time (⊠ 1586 Market St., ☎ 415/553–8900), an art deco lover's delight, carries furniture and accessories by Heywood Wakefield and others. It's conveniently close to a whole host of other stores that stock vintage collectibles.

Cinema Shop (⊠ 606 Geary St., ☎ 415/885–6785), a 25-year-old tiny storefront, is jammed with more than 250,000 original posters, stills, lobby cards, and rare videotapes of Hollywood classics and schlock films.

Held Over (⊠ 1543 Haight St., ☎ 415/864–0818) carries an extensive collection of clothing, accessories, shoes, handbags, and jewelry from the 1940s, '50s, and '60s.

San Francisco Rock Art and Collectibles (⊠ 1851 Powell St., ☎ 415/956–6759 or 800/949–1965) has a huge selection of rock-and-roll memorabilia, including posters, handbills, and original art. Also available are posters from recent shows—many at the legendary Fillmore Auditorium—with musicians like George Clinton, Porno for Pyros, and Johnny Cash.

The Schlep Sisters (⌧ 4327 18th St., ☎ 415/626–0581) has a fine selection of secondhand American dinnerware, art pottery, and glass, as well as 1950s home accessories such as cookie jars and salt-and-pepper shakers.

INDEX

WHEREVER YOU TRAVEL, *H*ELP IS NEVER FAR AWAY.

From planning your trip to providing travel assistance along the way, American Express® Travel Service Offices are always there to help you do more.

San Francisco

American Express Travel Service
455 Market Street
415/536-2600

American Express Travel Service
560 California Street
415/536-2600

Ethan Allen Travel, Inc. (R)
1585 Sloat Boulevard
415/242-0277